The
Social
Kitchen

The Social Kitchen

Food for family & friends   SHALLY TUCKER

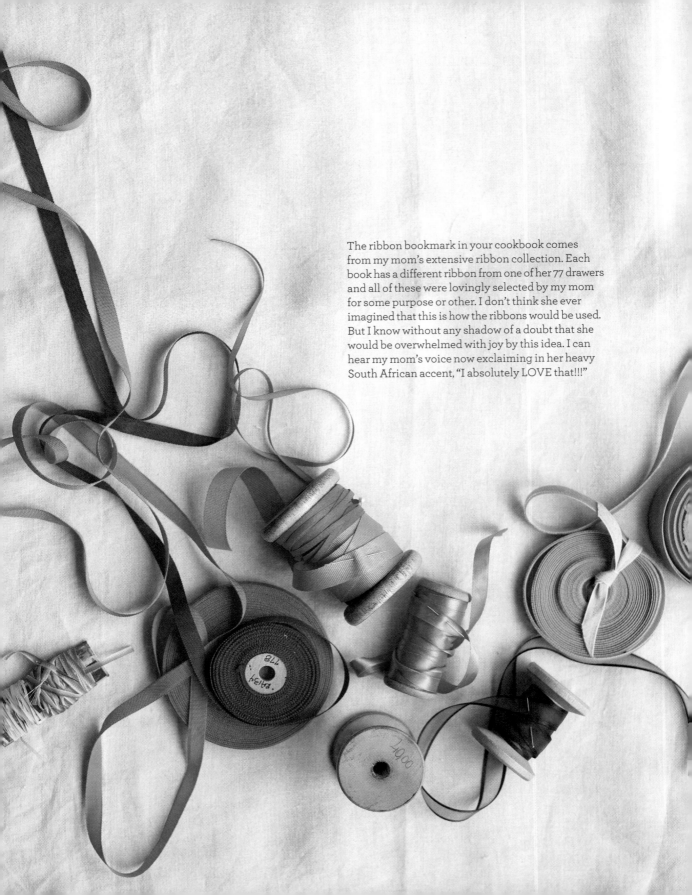

The ribbon bookmark in your cookbook comes from my mom's extensive ribbon collection. Each book has a different ribbon from one of her 77 drawers and all of these were lovingly selected by my mom for some purpose or other. I don't think she ever imagined that this is how the ribbons would be used. But I know without any shadow of a doubt that she would be overwhelmed with joy by this idea. I can hear my mom's voice now exclaiming in her heavy South African accent, "I absolutely LOVE that!!!"

"A" is our family secret code. It's the way we say "I love you," "We're okay," and " I'm right here for you" to one another.

Its origin is as mysterious as its use. My parents used it to reassure each other that there was nothing or no-one they loved more than each other. They signed off their letters with "A", they ended phone conversations this way, and they would often just whisper it quietly in a crowded, noisy room.

"A" is the Tucker family symbol of love, hope and strength.

Photography: Dan Jones
Additional photography: Andrew Burton
Project editor: Jinny Johnson
Design: Smith & Gilmour
Food styling: Charlie Clapp
Additional food styling: Christina Mackenzie
Prop styling: Linda Berlin
Photographer's assistants: Sophie Fox,
Simon Mackenzie
Proofreader: Constance Novis
Indexer: Vicki Robinson

Colour origination by Altaimage Ltd
Printed and bound in Italy by L.E.G.O.

www.thesocialkitchen.org
@the_social_kitchen

The recipes
These recipes have come from the many
notes and cuttings Shally kept over the years.
She always put her own individual stamp on
anything she cooked, but we wholeheartedly
apologise if you feel that any recipe belongs
to you, and we hope you will forgive us.

Contents

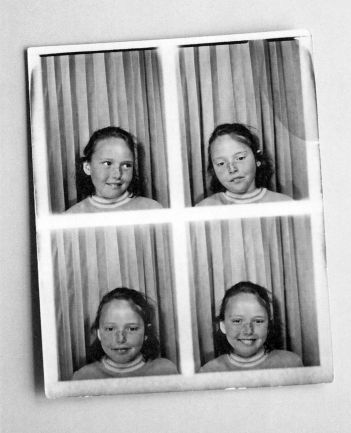

Foreword

It's no secret that Sharon (Shally) suffered from a number of auto-immune diseases, the most disabling of which were psoriasis and psoriatic arthritis. Not only did she have to contend with sore, burning red skin, which at times could become pustular, but she also had severely painful swollen joints and tendons that made movement difficult and sleep nearly impossible. Medicines administered to control the inflammatory processes often led to infections and complications caused by suppression of her immune system.

There are more than 2,000 skin diseases, many of them life-threatening. Dermatrust is a registered charity, which was established to improve the care of patients like Sharon, to fund research to identify the underlying causes of skin disease and to develop new treatments for them. The Trustees are particularly targeting skin cancer, which is the commonest cancer in the world, as well as inflammatory skin diseases like Sharon's, which make normal daily life impossible.

There is now a new Institute of Immunity and Transplantation at the Royal Free Hospital and an academic department of Skin Immunology has been established, with the support of Dermatrust. The Trustees believe that these scientists and academics, all working towards a common goal, will provide the opportunity to develop new treatments for eczema, psoriasis, skin cancer and connective tissue diseases. All of these conditions have an immune basis and affect millions of people worldwide.

Sharon and her family have been promoting and assisting Dermatrust for many years, and the Trustees of Dermatrust are so grateful that the proceeds of *The Social Kitchen* will help to further our research goals. Enjoy following the recipes to create delicious food with the knowledge that your purchase raises valuable funds, allowing our scientists to develop breakthroughs in the treatment of life-changing skin diseases.

Professor Malcolm Rustin
Chairman of Trustees
Dermatrust

This One's For You, Mom

During the last week of my mother's life I did not leave her side. After so many visits and years of care, the doctors and nurses at the hospital had become part of our family and they accommodated us so that we could be as close to our mom as possible. Those final days of her life were the most difficult she had ever experienced. She had fought her illnesses for so long and she had such a fierce will to live that she had defied her precarious and difficult situation.

Our family fought with her and for her and we were always right beside her. But in those last days it was clear that she was in excruciating pain and totally exhausted. It was not that she had given up – she was not a woman who gave up on anything – but she had come to terms with her situation and we knew there was no other option. During that time something felt different to all the other critical moments we had experienced. We knew and understood that there really was nothing more anyone could do for my mother. We were only grateful that we were prepared, and that she was leaving us so gracefully.

I left the hospital only once over that time to meet some friends for coffee and to get some fresh air. The moment I sat down I received the dreaded phone call to return to the hospital. I jumped into a cab and headed back, knowing what lay before me. My mother wanted to say goodbye. She called each of us in, one by one. It was her time to thank us, to bless, hug and love us one last time. Many people miss the opportunity of a final farewell and it was so important to us.

This was the most profound moment of my life so far. There was an awesome sense of closure and a deep feeling of peace. My greatest fear had been that my mother would die alone, but instead she died in the loving embrace of her husband, children, parents, siblings and friends. She died as she had lived – surrounded by love.

A friend of my mother's took me home from the hospital. I'd not been back for some time and my plan was to run in, quickly grab some clothes to wear to the funeral and head directly to my parents' home. But as I walked into my house I saw on my dining room table, lying obviously and comfortably as though they'd always been there, my mother's hand-written cookbooks. These leather-bound black books were overflowing with her favourite recipes, notes, a pinch of salt here and a dash of sugar there. The books were filled with scraps of paper and memories, reflecting her passionate relationship with food and her love of anything beautiful, colourful and creative. There were recipes reaching as far back as my great-grandmothers on both sides – a legacy of deliciousness.

To this day I have no idea how these books arrived in my home, but I now know why they came there. I knew then very vaguely what I know now for sure. I had to use them to honour my mother's passion for food and for life.

For her, it was not only about dishes and tastes but also about bringing people together. My mother loved to have a home overflowing with friends – the food was there to add to the magic, to nourish and to indulge. Friends were constantly arriving, seeking guidance and advice, support and insight but mostly just to be near to my mother, to be inspired by her endless joie de vivre and comforted by her wisdom. Our home was an oasis of light and laughter – a proverbial shelter from the storm.

Some visitors stayed for a couple of hours, others for a couple of months. Every person who entered our home left feeling better – and fuller. At the heart of all this was my mother, sitting firmly at our kitchen table. In fact, after many occasions when we set a formal table in our dining room only to find guests clinging to the kitchen table, my mother decided to bring the dining room to the kitchen and so we had two large tables in our kitchen – and, of course, a very social kitchen.

And so, the social kitchen that my mother created in our home is now a credit to her. This book is a testament to her, to her life's work, to the adoration of her family and friends. Nowadays when people ask me how I've been doing since my mom's death I answer as honestly as I know how. Every day is difficult but I live with the intention of attempting to emulate her vivacious nature. I want to honour her struggle but more importantly to honour her courage, fortitude and energy for life.

When my mother cooked it was always for a crowd. She felt her way through recipes with a haphazard but instinctive sense of knowing what worked. She cooked by taste and with love. In order to translate her quixotic ways into a cookbook detailing precise methods and measures has been a delightful but challenging journey. The recipes the book contains reflect our South African and Jewish roots, our Lithuanian heritage and our English upbringing – the eclectic mixture of our home and our food.

The proceeds of this book will go to charity. This was my mother's way – she was charitable, generous, kind and always thinking of others. She insisted that kindness is an endless process that ripples beyond our imagination. My hope is that this cookbook will bring as much joy into your homes and dishes as my mother brought to ours. And may the proceeds ensure that those who are suffering are easily healed.

Love Dani x

Shally's Life

My mother, Sharon Leigh Rapp, was born on 14 September 1960 in Johannesburg. Her parents, Michael and Maureen Rapp, had three children: Ira, Sharon and Craig. Her older brother Ira found it hard to say the name Sharon Leigh so she became Shally from then on. In the 1960s Michael and Maureen divorced and Michael married Phyllis, who had two children from her previous marriage. Michael and Phyllis went on to have one more child, Jody, bringing the family to a total of six children.

Shally matriculated in 1977, and in 1978 began Hotel School in Johannesburg, where she studied Industrial Catering. There she met Lawrence Tucker, the love of her life and future husband.

At the end of 1979 Lawrence won a scholarship to the Savoy Hotel in London and my parents decided to leave South Africa for promising prospects in the UK. At the time they weren't married and knew only one other person living in the city – one of mom's closest friends from school, Laura Daniel.

During this first year in London Shally worked with Prue Leith as a chef at the Kuwait Investment Office, but in February 1981 she and Lawrence decided to head back to South Africa to get married. After working for a while, taking on lots of catering jobs around Johannesburg, they were married on 16 August 1981. They had a one-night honeymoon at the Mount Nelson Hotel in Cape Town, then returned to London almost immediately to start their married life.

Back in London, Shally and Lawrence bought the Bentinck House Hotel, on Bentinck Street, W1. It had 26 bedrooms and they did everything, from the cleaning of the rooms to cooking for all the guests. A year later they decided to expand and they acquired the Diplomat Hotel in Belgravia, which had 38 rooms. They worked tirelessly, side-by-side, building their business.

In 1983 their first child Danielle (Dani) was born. That same year Ira, Shally's older brother, moved to London and bought into the business; together they acquired the Westside Express Restaurant in Harrods.

In 1985 they had their second child, Ryan. The rest of Shally's immediate family arrived in London and joined Lawrence and Shally's enterprise, which rapidly expanded to include a property business.

I was born in 1989 and when I was only six months old my mother started to fall ill. She was diagnosed with psoriasis and was put on medication, but unfortunately her condition did not improve and developed into pustular psoriasis.

Mom was taken into the Wellington Hospital in St John's Wood, London. She spent three months in intensive care fighting for her life – she had 100 per cent coverage of pustular psoriasis. Yet somehow she managed to pull through. Her case was one of the rarest ever witnessed at that time, but the doctors were eventually able to control her symptoms, allowing her to live as normal a life as possible, despite having to battle so dire an illness.

In 1992 Shally opened an arts and crafts shop, called Outstamping, in Edgware. People still come up to us and tell us how much they loved that shop and how much our mother inspired them, but she eventually had to sell the business as it was becoming too time consuming. She wanted to spend more time with the family. What is more, she was becoming sicker and didn't have the energy to cope with the shop.

In 2000 mom's illness worsened and she needed more and more care. My parents decided to sell everything so that my dad could look after Shally full-time. In 2011 my mom suffered multiple organ failure and went into a coma for almost two weeks. On 25 November 2013, exactly two years later, my mom passed away.

The last five years of her life were the most difficult. She fought courageously and had to have many daily injections and copious amounts of pills. She was on oxygen for up to 24 hours a day and had to have intravenous antibiotic drips and feeding tubes.

There's no doubt in our minds that my mother would not have lived as long as she did without the help of her doctors, led by Professor Rustin, and the nurses at the King Edward VII Hospital, all of whom treated her with the utmost dignity and respect.

Megs

Soups & Starters

Chicken Soup

SERVES 8–10
1 large free-range chicken
5 medium carrots, peeled
  and roughly chopped
1 large onion, peeled and
  roughly chopped
salt and black pepper

This is a staple in any Jewish home and often served with perogen (see page 19). Mom would use all sorts of vegetables to make a lovely rich-flavoured broth, so add whatever you fancy. Great way to clear the fridge too.

Put the chicken in a large stockpot or saucepan and half fill the pan with cold water. Put a lid on the pan and slowly bring the water to the boil. Take the lid off the pan from time to time and skim off any foamy scum that appears on the surface with a slotted spoon.

Once the water has come to a gentle simmer, add the carrots and onion to the pan. Put the lid on again, bring the water back to a simmer and leave the soup to tick away on a low heat for 2 hours.

At the end of the 2 hours, carefully remove the chicken, put it on a plate and leave it to cool slightly. Using a couple of forks, shred the meat off the bones. Keep about 100 grams of meat for making perogen (see p. 19) and put the rest back in the pan.

You can serve the soup as it is or pour everything into a big bowl and leave it in the fridge overnight. In the morning, skim off any fat that's risen to the surface and chuck it away.

When you're ready to eat, warm the soup through again, add salt and pepper to taste and serve it with the perogen. If you prefer, you can strain the soup through a sieve to make a rich, clear broth.

Perogen

MAKES 12
1 tbsp vegetable oil
½ small onion, peeled
    and finely chopped
100g cooked chicken,
    finely chopped
2 sprigs of thyme, leaves
    picked from the stems
½ packet Osem onion soup
    powder (optional)
1 tbsp plain flour, plus
    extra for rolling
300g all-butter puff pastry
1 egg
black pepper

We serve perogen alongside chicken soup so everyone can add them to the soup or just dunk them in. And you don't have to eat them with soup – we all love them just as they are, as a snack. Osem soup powder was an ingredient mom used a lot. It's an Israeli product but you can buy it everywhere now. We always made loads of perogen at a time and it would be all hands on deck for rolling, filling and folding; a real conveyor belt operation.

Preheat the oven to 200°C/Fan 180°C/Gas 6. Line a baking tray with baking parchment or foil.

Heat the oil in a frying pan over a medium heat and gently fry the onion for 8–10 minutes until it's soft. Add the cooked chicken to the pan with the thyme, onion soup powder, flour and a glass of water – about 200ml is fine. Stir the mixture well, then allow it to bubble and thicken for 5 minutes. Season with plenty of pepper – and if you're not using onion soup powder add some salt as well. Tip everything into a bowl and leave it to cool.

Lightly sprinkle your work surface with flour. Roll out the pastry to a thickness of about 2mm, turning it often so it doesn't stick to the surface. Using a 9cm cutter, cut out 12 circles of pastry. Break the egg into a small bowl and beat it lightly.

Put a dollop of filling on each pastry circle, then brush round the edges of the pastry with the beaten egg. Fold the pastry over to enclose the filling and press the edges well with your fingers, then with a fork to seal them.

Brush the perogen with beaten egg, place them on the baking tray and bake in the hot oven for 15–20 minutes until golden brown and puffed up.

If Only Our Table Could Talk

· * · *

We grew up in a South African-inspired 'madhouse' in London where my parents were constantly entertaining family and friends. The number of guests would range anywhere from two to a casual 50 or so. Our friends would turn up at all hours of the day with the understanding that there was always something to eat – and there always was. There might be anything from cakes or salads to roast dinners, but one thing was always certain – no-one would leave hungry.

Our mother had her firm spot at our kitchen table. Despite her challenges, she was always busy making and creating something. But, she never did anything alone. If friends intended to come and have a quick cup of tea; they would inevitably end up staying all day to help roll out dough or chop vegetables. Mom had the ability to include, create, empathize and listen. Our kitchen table bears the tears and joys of all of our friends and family. It holds the tribulations and triumphs that were quietly revealed to our mother while she was preparing something delicious for everyone to enjoy.

Our mother's kitchen is still the soul of our home. Our kitchen table is ingrained with mom's energy and effervescent personality. It was the surface upon which her philosophy lived: to encourage people to cook, to enjoy life, to give back, to entertain, to create and to have fun. That table withstood my mother's wisdom, creativity, humour and quirky ideologies – all of which built the foundations of our home and family. My mother always used to say "If only our table could talk." Our standard response would be "It's better that it doesn't."

Mom's Vegetable Soup

SERVES 8–10
3 tbsp olive oil
1 onion, peeled and
    roughly chopped
2 medium leeks,
    roughly chopped
2 celery sticks,
    roughly chopped
2 medium courgettes,
    roughly chopped
1 small butternut squash,
    peeled and roughly
    chopped
1 large waxy potato, peeled
    and roughly chopped
1 turnip (or 8 baby turnips),
    peeled and roughly
    chopped
1 litre chicken stock
salt and black pepper

This is a favourite winter soup for our family as it warms you up beautifully. Make it chunky or as smooth and velvety as baby food – whatever you prefer.

Heat the oil in a large saucepan over a medium heat. Add the onion, leeks, celery sticks and courgettes and cook them gently for 15 minutes, stirring often.

Add the squash, potato and turnip to the pan and keep cooking for another 5 minutes. Add the stock, bring to a simmer and leave the soup to bubble away gently for about 30 minutes until all the vegetables are soft.

Use a stick blender to blitz the soup briefly. Don't over-process it, as this soup is best quite rough-textured, not too smooth. Add salt and pepper to taste and serve with some good crusty bread.

Red Soup

SERVES 8–10
3 tbsp olive oil, plus
    extra for drizzling
1 red onion, peeled and
    roughly chopped
3 garlic cloves, peeled
    and roughly chopped
2 celery sticks, roughly
    chopped
2 medium carrots, peeled
    and roughly chopped
400g can of butter beans
500ml chicken or
    vegetable stock
2 x 400g cans of chopped
    tomatoes
2 large ripe fresh tomatoes,
    roughly chopped
¼ savoy cabbage,
    finely sliced
100g fresh or frozen peas
salt and black pepper

The vivid colour of this soup makes it very enticing and it's so easy to make. It keeps well in the fridge for several days or you can freeze it for up to two months. Perfect for a quick meal.

Heat the 3 tablespoons of olive oil in a large saucepan and add the onion, garlic, celery and carrots. Cook them gently over a medium heat for 10 minutes until everything is soft and sweet.

Tip the butter beans into the pan – juice and all – and add the stock and the canned tomatoes. Bring the soup to the boil, then add the fresh tomatoes and the cabbage. Simmer gently for 25 minutes, add the peas and cook for a further 5 minutes until everything is tender.

Season to taste, then ladle the hot soup into bowls and drizzle with a swirl of olive oil before serving.

Cabbage Soup

SERVES 6
1 leek, cleaned
  and finely sliced
1 carrot, peeled and
  roughly chopped
1 celery stick,
  roughly chopped
6 medium tomatoes,
  roughly chopped
4 beef short ribs
3 tbsp apricot jam
1 large green cabbage
  (such as Savoy),
  finely sliced
salt and black pepper

Adding beef short ribs makes this into a really meaty meal of a soup. The meat is cooked until it's falling off the bone and soft and delicious.

Throw the leek, carrot, celery and tomatoes into a large pan with the ribs and apricot jam. Add the finely sliced cabbage and about 2 litres of water (or enough to cover the ribs). Bring the water to the boil, then skim off any scum that floats to the surface. Put a lid on the pan and leave the soup to simmer away gently for about 4 hours. By this time the meat should be falling off the ribs and the soup should be rich and tasty.

Skim off any fat that's risen to the top, remove the bones and season to taste. Serve in big bowls with crusty bread.

Knochen

SERVES 6

4 carrots, peeled
2 celery sticks
500g beef bones
    with marrow
200g pearl barley
salt and black pepper

"While my family back in London is busy putting together this beautiful book of Shally's recipes, I am on a ship, heading for Antarctica. I'm remembering something that Shally used to do that I loved so much. Whenever I visited her on a cold, grey winter's day in London and needed warming up, she would cook me a very special soup called *knochen*. It was made from beef marrow bones and it was perfect. I loved it and I loved that she made it just for me. Here on the other side of the world, I'm craving the comforting warmth of that soup. At our next port of call the ship's chef is going to try and find some of those bones and cook up a big pot of *knochen*. When we're in the Antarctic and coming back on board after a day exploring in the freezing cold, we will eat that special soup and I will think of Shally, my beloved daughter." (Mike)

Roughly chop the carrots and celery and put them in a large saucepan with the beef bones. Add 3 litres of cold water. Place on the hob and bring to a simmer, then carefully skim any scum from the surface.

Put a lid on the pan and let the soup boil gently for about 2 hours. Add the pearl barley and continue to cook the soup for a further hour. Season to taste, then serve.

Brown Onion Soup

25g unsalted butter
2 tbsp olive oil
5 large onions, peeled
    and finely sliced
1 beef or vegetable
    stock cube
2 tbsp brown sugar
2 tbsp plain flour, sifted
1 tbsp Dijon mustard
250g crusty bread, torn
    into rough chunks
50g Gruyère cheese,
    grated
salt and black pepper

We generally just ladle soup out from the pan on the stove, but we like to serve this onion soup at the table from a big casserole dish. It looks amazing!

Add the butter and oil to a large casserole dish and place it over a medium heat until the butter has melted. Add the onions and stir them well so they are all nicely coated in the fat. Put a lid on the casserole and sweat the onions for 30 minutes, stirring frequently. You want them to turn a lovely golden colour, so leave them a little longer if need be.

Preheat the oven to 200°C/Fan 180°C/Gas 6. Crumble the stock cube over the onions and sprinkle in the sugar, then add the flour, mustard and a good pinch of salt and pepper. Increase the heat slightly and continue to cook for a few minutes until the onions are a gorgeously thick, sticky mass. Add 1 litre of hot water, and stir, then bring the soup to the boil. Put a lid on the casserole, pop it in the oven and bake for about an hour.

Take the casserole out of the oven and preheat your grill to high. Take the lid off and scatter the chunks of bread over the soup. Sprinkle the cheese on top, then place the casserole under the grill for 5 minutes or so or until the cheese is bubbling and golden. Take the casserole to the table, ladle the soup into bowls and enjoy. Nice with some extra bread on the side.

Baked Asparagus with Crisps

SERVES 8–10

750g asparagus
50g butter
50g plain flour
50g Cheddar cheese,
    grated
1 lemon
50g cheese and
    onion crisps
vegetable oil
salt and white pepper

Cheese and onion crisps are our family favourite for the topping on this dish, but experiment with the flavours you love best, such as cracked black pepper or chilli.

Preheat the oven to 200°C/Fan 180°C/Gas 6. Trim off the tough woody ends of the asparagus.

Bring a pan of water to the boil, season it with salt, then add the asparagus and blanch it for 2 minutes. Making sure you keep that lovely flavourful cooking water, drain the asparagus and put it in a medium-sized ovenproof dish.

Melt the butter in a small saucepan over a medium heat, then stir in the flour. Gradually add the asparagus cooking water, stirring constantly so the sauce doesn't go lumpy. Boil the sauce for a couple of minutes while stirring, then take the pan off the heat. Season the sauce with a pinch of salt and some white pepper, then add half the grated cheese and a squeeze of lemon juice to taste.

Crush the crisps and scatter them over the top with the rest of the grated cheese, then drizzle with a little oil. Bake the asparagus in the hot oven for 10–20 minutes until the topping is golden brown.

The Tuckers' Farm

∗·∗

When mom got so sick she couldn't go shopping as often, she took to the Internet and we would get loads of random deliveries at the house. One day, about 50 boxes of metal farm animals created from recycled oil drums arrived. There were dogs, roosters, ducks, all sorts, made in Australia. She'd seen them on a website, loved them and bought loads. It was cheaper to keep them than to send them back.

We just had to laugh at these things, now placed all over the house and garden. Oscar and Mac, our golden cocker spaniels, took time to get used to them, as they felt their territory had been invaded. The animals are the first things you notice when walking through our purple front door and they remind everyone of mom's quirkiness – our home is overflowing with things that she admired and had to have. And she always found a place for everything, including a farmyard of metal animals from across the globe.

Creamy Spinach Dip

SERVES 8-10
500g fresh or frozen
   spinach
225g can of water
   chestnuts, finely
   chopped
200g crème fraîche
150ml soured cream
1 tbsp Osem vegetable
   soup powder or
   bouillon powder
2 spring onions,
   finely chopped
2 medium challah
   breads (see p.39)

This dip is so good and really easy to make. It's great served with challah, which you can buy or make yourself (see page 39), or enjoy it with some crisps or crackers.

Wash the spinach, if using fresh, or defrost frozen spinach. Put the spinach in a large pan and cook it gently over a low heat for 5 minutes. Drain and leave the spinach to cool slightly, then squeeze out as much water as you can.

Chop the spinach finely, then put it in a bowl with the water chestnuts, crème fraîche, soured cream and the soup or bouillon powder. Give everything a good stir, then mix in the spring onions.

Take a challah bread and hollow out an oval in the centre. Pile the spinach mixture into this space. Break up the bread you've pulled out, and the remaining challah, and arrange them around the filled challah for everyone to use to scoop up the delicious dip. You can eat this straightaway or leave it overnight in the fridge.

Challah

MAKES 4 LARGE
CHALLAH
1 litre lukewarm water
230g sugar
20g dried yeast
4 eggs
235ml vegetable oil
1 tbsp salt
1.5–2kg flour

For sweet challah
2 tbsp agave nectar
3 tbsp golden syrup
light brown soft sugar,
    for sprinkling

We always found that if you're making challah you might as well make a few, so we would bake loads and give them to our guests. The plaiting part is quite creative and spiritual, and if someone is sick you say a prayer while you make the challah. If you like, you can freeze the dough and the baked loaves.

Pour the lukewarm water into a large bowl, add the sugar and yeast and stir them to dissolve. Leave it for a while until the yeast starts to bubble. Crack 3 of the eggs into a bowl and beat well.

Add the oil, salt, and beaten eggs to the yeast mixture, then slowly add the flour a little at a time. You might not need it all – even just a kilo might be enough. Knead the dough well until it has a smooth consistency, the cover the bowl with a tea towel and leave it in a warm place to rise for 4–5 hours. It may quadruple in size. Preheat the oven to 200°C/Fan 180°C/Gas 6.

Punch the dough down to get rid of any air pockets, then divide the dough into 4 pieces. Cut each of these into 4 again and shape them into long strands of equal length.

To shape each challah, lay down 4 strands, pinch them together at the top, then plait them neatly. Everyone has their own ideas about plaiting, but you can experiment and have fun coming up with your own designs. Beat the remaining egg in a bowl and use it to brush the challah.

Bake the challah for 30–40 minutes. To check that it's done, tap the bottom – it should sound hollow.

SWEET CHALLAH

Make as above, adding the agave nectar and golden syrup after the oil. When you've brushed the challah with beaten egg , sprinkle it with the sugar before putting it in the oven.

Chopped Herring

SERVES 8–10
3 large eggs
3 x 240g jars of pickled
   herrings or rollmop
   herrings, drained
1 onion, peeled and
   finely chopped.
1 green apple, peeled,
   cored and finely
   chopped
4 Digestive biscuits

You can make your own pickled herrings for this (see page 44) or use jars of herrings for a really quick dish.

Bring a small pan of water to the boil, add the eggs and simmer them for 8–10 minutes. Drain, then run the eggs under cold water until they're completely cool – this helps to prevent that nasty grey ring that can appear around the yolks. Peel the eggs.

Put 2 of the eggs in a food processor and add the drained herrings, onion, apple and biscuits. Pulse until you have a mixture with a nice smooth consistency, then taste it and add a little more of the herring vinegar if you like.

Scoop the mixture out on to a serving plate. Separate the yolk and white of the remaining egg and finely chop them both. Scatter them over the chopped herring and serve with kichel (see p.43) or challah (see p.39).

Kichel

250ml sunflower oil,
    plus extra for oiling
    and brushing
4 medium eggs
250g caster sugar, plus
    extra for sprinkling
pinch of salt
500g self-raising flour,
    plus extra for rolling

Kichel are a classic Jewish South African favourite and they go beautifully with chopped herring or chopped liver. With our help, mom always made lots so that we could give everyone some to take home. We got the process down to a fine art and could make 300 kichel in two hours.

Preheat the oven to 200°C/Fan 180°C/Gas 6. Brush a little of the oil over a wire cooling rack, then place the rack on a baking sheet and leave it aside until needed.

Crack the eggs into a large bowl and beat them with the rest of the oil, the sugar and salt until everything is well mixed together. Slowly add the flour until you have a good workable dough.

Bring the dough together with your hands, then tip it on to a lightly floured work surface. Knead the dough for a couple of minutes until it's smooth and soft.

Roll out the dough to a thickness of 1–2mm. It's best to use a pasta machine for doing this, reducing the setting each time you roll the dough through until it is at its thinnest.

Using the crinkly edge of a 7.5cm cookie cutter cut the dough into rounds.

Place the rounds on the oiled rack, making sure they're not too close together as they will spread a little. You'll probably need to cook them in a couple of batches so you don't overcrowd the rack.

Brush the kichel with a bit more oil and sprinkle them with sugar, then bake in the oven for 5 minutes until they're slightly golden and crisp. Remove them from the rack and leave them to cool while you cook the rest.

Pickled Herrings

MAKES 12

12 large fresh herring
  fillets, skin on
50g salt
200ml white wine
200ml white wine vinegar
3 or 4 bay leaves
2 small onions, peeled
  and finely sliced
  into rounds
½ tsp fennel seeds
1 tsp allspice berries
1 tsp black peppercorns
1 tsp white peppercorns
1 strip of finely pared
  lemon zest

Ask your fishmonger to fillet and pinbone the herrings and that's all the hard work done. To sterilize jars, wash them well in hot, soapy water or in the dishwasher. Heat the oven to 140°C/Fan 120°C/Gas 1. Put the jars on a baking sheet, then pop them in the oven until they are completely dry. Remove them carefully – they will be hot!

Check that the herring fillets are neatly trimmed and remove any little bones that remain. Pour 500ml of cold water into a bowl, add the salt and let it dissolve. Add the fillets and leave them in the brine for a couple of hours.

Put the remaining ingredients in a medium saucepan, bring them to the boil, and then simmer for a minute or so. Take the pan off the heat and set aside and leave the mixture to cool.

Drain the herring fillets, rinse them carefully and pat them dry with kitchen towel. Roll them up, skin-side facing out, and secure with a wooden toothpick. Pack the herrings into 3 or 4 medium-sized, sterilized jars, then pour the cooled marinade over them. Seal the jars.

Store the herrings in the fridge for 2 days to give the flavours a chance to develop. If you want a softer, more pickled rollmop, leave them for a few more days, as the longer you leave them the softer they get. Serve with bread and butter, chopped dill and kichel (see p. 43).

Pickled Onions

SERVES 6

4 medium onions
½ tsp peppercorns
1 tsp mustard seeds
1 tsp salt
1 tbsp caster sugar
300ml malt vinegar
300ml water

You can buy pickled onions anywhere of course, but somehow the ones we make at home are much sweeter and nicer. So easy to do, too.

Peel the onions and slice them thinly into half moons. Soak the onion slices in a bowl of salted just-boiled water for 5 minutes, then drain them and rinse in cold water. Pack the onions into clean sterilized jars.

Mix the remaining ingredients together, add 300ml of water and pour the mixture over the onions to cover. Put the lid on and leave for a few days, but the longer you leave the onions, the better they taste.

Danish Herrings with Apples

SERVES 8–10

4 x 240g jars of herrings
    or homemade pickled
    herrings (see p.44)
250g sugar
200ml oil
250ml brown vinegar
2 firm apples, peeled,
    cored and diced
1 white onion, peeled
    and thinly sliced
1 tsp mustard powder
¼ tsp black pepper
200g tomato purée

Our dad doesn't eat fish, but he loves the sauce from this recipe. He just eats it by itself or soaks it up with a bit of bread. This dish is best made a day or so before you want to serve it so the flavours can develop.

Drain the herrings and cut them into pieces. Mix all the other ingredients in a big bowl, then add the herrings. Leave for day or so in the fridge, then serve with challah (see p.39) or crusty bread.

Fish Torte & Pink Horseradish Sauce

SERVES 8–10

vegetable oil
1kg white fish fillets
    (such as cod)
1 large carrot, peeled
    and cut into chunks
240ml vegetable oil
185g matzo meal
150g sugar
½ tsp mustard powder
1 tsp garlic salt

Pink horseradish sauce
125ml chrane
125ml mayonnaise

This bright pink sauce is made with chrane, which is a mixture of horseradish sauce and beetroot, and is completely delicious. You can buy it in Jewish stores or make your own very easily (see below).

Grease a 20cm springform cake tin with oil. Preheat the oven to 200°C/Fan 180°C/Gas 6.

Rinse the fish and cut it into medium-sized chunks. Put the fish and the chunks of carrot into a food processor and blitz until minced.

Tip the mixture into a bowl and add the remaining ingredients – except the sauce – and 240ml of water, then stir well. Spoon everything into the cake tin and bake for 40–60 minutes until set. Remove the torte from the oven and leave it to cool, then turn it on to a plate.

Mix the chrane with the mayo to make the pink horseradish sauce and serve it on the side.

CHRANE

To make your own chrane, chop 3 large cooked beetroot and put them in a food processor with 2 teaspoons of horseradish sauce and 1 teaspoon of sugar. Whizz it all up and it's ready to use.

Chopped Liver

SERVES 8–10

8 large eggs
4 tbsp sunflower oil
2 onions, peeled and
    finely sliced
750g chicken livers
1 tsp simulated chicken
    fat (optional)
salt and black pepper

Buy organic chicken livers if you can or the best quality you can find. If you're in a rush and don't have time to chop the livers by hand, put them in a food processor or through a mincer.

Bring a small pan of water to the boil, add the eggs and simmer them for 8–10 minutes. Drain and run the eggs under cold water until they're completely cool, then peel them and chop them roughly.

Heat a tablespoon of the oil in a frying pan over a medium heat and cook the onions for 10 minutes until they're soft and translucent. Scoop the onions out of the pan with a slotted spoon and put them on a plate.

Add another tablespoon of the oil to the pan and fry the livers over a high heat for 8–10 minutes or until they're golden and very nearly cooked. Carefully drain off any excess liquid from the pan. Put the onions back in the pan with the livers and continue to cook for another 5 minutes until the livers are cooked through. Take the pan off the heat and leave the livers to cool slightly.

Put the eggs on a chopping board with the livers (and onion) and a good pinch of salt and pepper. Finely chop or mash everything together, then if it looks a bit dry, add a teaspoon of simulated chicken fat. Serve with kichel (p.43) or challah (p.39).

Hot Pickled Peppers with Cream Cheese & Za'atar Pitta Chips

SERVES 6–8
3 large yellow peppers
3 large red peppers
250ml red wine vinegar
200g granulated sugar
4 pitta breads
olive oil, for drizzling
2 tsp za'atar
250g soft cream cheese

If you make more peppers than you need, the leftovers keep well in a sterilized jar and can be served on toast, in a salad or a tart or however you fancy. By the way, za'atar is a Middle Eastern spice mixture containing thyme, sesame seeds, salt and sumac.

Remove the seeds from the peppers and slice the flesh into 1cm strips. It's best not to cut them any thinner than that, as the strips do shrink a little in the vinegar and you want lots of lovely crunch and texture.

Put the vinegar and sugar in a saucepan with 500ml of water and gently bring to the boil, stirring to dissolve the sugar. Once the sugar has dissolved, add the sliced peppers and simmer them gently for 1–2 hours until most of the liquid has gone and the peppers are sticky and caramelized. Tip them into a bowl and leave them to cool slightly while you cook the pitta chips.

Preheat the oven to 200°C/Fan 180°C/Gas 6. Slice the pitta breads into fingers. Drizzle them with olive oil, then sprinkle on the za'atar and toss until they are all well covered. Spread the pitta chips on a baking sheet and bake them for 5 minutes until they're beginning to crisp.

Gently whip the cream cheese until it's soft, then dollop it on to the centre of a serving dish. Pour the hot peppers and their sticky pickling juices on to the cream cheese. Serve with pitta chips and enjoy.

Onion Tart

SERVES 8

Pastry
250g flour
½ tsp salt
125g cold butter, cubed
3–4 tbsp milk
1 egg, beaten

Filling
25g butter
1 tbsp olive oil
8 onions, peeled
   and finely sliced
100ml double cream
3 eggs
25g Cheddar
   cheese, grated
25g Parmesan
   cheese, grated
salt and black pepper

You can make a big tart like the one in the picture or lots of little bite-size ones in a mini-muffin tray. Cook the small ones for about 15 minutes.

First make the pastry. Sift the flour and salt into a large bowl. Add the cubes of butter, then rub them into the flour, working them between your fingers and thumb until the mixture is the consistency of coarse breadcrumbs and has yellowed slightly. Alternatively, sift the flour into a food processor, add the butter and blitz.

Add the milk and mix it in with a knife, then tip the lot on to a lightly floured work surface and knead once or twice to combine. Roll the pastry out into a circle large enough to fit your dish with a little to spare – a loose-bottomed tart tin or an ovenproof baking dish would be fine. Carefully transfer the pastry to the tin or dish and press it into the edges. Cut off any pastry overhanging the edges with a sharp knife, making sure you leave ½ cm proud of the edge. Prick the pastry all over with a fork, then pop it into the fridge to rest for 20 minutes while you make the filling.

Heat the butter and oil in a large pan over a medium heat. Add the onions and stir well to coat them all in fat, then put a lid on the pan. Cook the onions for 30–45 minutes until they are really soft and caramelized all over, stirring often. Season them well and set aside.

Preheat the oven to 200°C/Fan 180°C/Gas 6. Put a piece of baking parchment over the pastry in the tin and fill with dried beans, rice or baking beans. Put the pastry case in the oven to bake for 10 minutes, then remove the beans and baking parchment and pop the pastry back in the oven for a further 5 minutes. Brush the sides and base with a little beaten egg to seal.

Mix the onions with the cream and eggs and season with salt and black pepper. Pour the mixture into the pastry case, sprinkle the cheeses on top and bake the tart for 30 minutes until it is golden and set.

Seventy-seven Drawers

* · *

Our mom was always busy with her hands. She was never without some knitting, sewing or something she was creating, and she had a huge collection of ribbons, fabric, sequins, buttons – anything unusual and beautiful. As she collected more and more bits and bobs she had to find somewhere to keep them all, so she bought this amazing chest of drawers she found in a shop in Islington.

She knew exactly what was in every one of those 77 little drawers. Something she loved to do was to take out one drawer at a time, sort through all the stuff and put it back. Mom could tell us about every individual object in those drawers; each had a story and a value. The smallest things in life brought her the greatest joy, and she used those pieces to enhance anything that was a little dull. Mom knew how to add a sparkle to life.

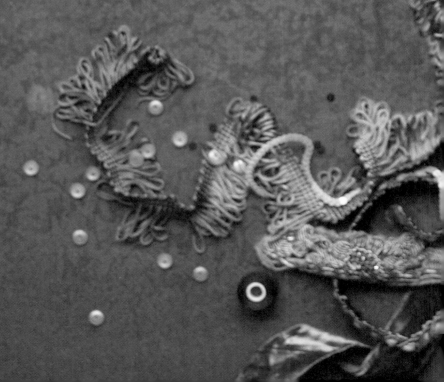

Salads & Veg

Tomato Salad

SERVES 8–10
1kg ripe heritage
   tomatoes
1 large red onion,
   finely sliced
3 tsp flaked sea salt
2 sprigs of fresh
   oregano, chopped
extra virgin olive oil
6 tbsp balsamic vinegar

It's the flavour of the tomatoes that makes this salad, so get really good tasty ones, such as heritage tomatoes, if you can. If you don't have any fresh oregano, hardy herbs such as rosemary or thyme also work well with the salt. Or just tear a few basil leaves over the tomatoes and toss them through.

Cut the tomatoes into slices or quarters and arrange them on a serving dish. Add the slices of red onion and mix them with the tomatoes.

Put the salt and oregano in a pestle and mortar and grind them together to create a lovely herbed salt.

Drizzle a good glug of oil over the tomatoes and onions and toss them well. Put the balsamic vinegar in a small saucepan and bring it to the boil over a high heat. Continue to boil it rapidly for 2 minutes until the balsamic has reduced to a nice thick glaze. Leave it to cool for a minute or so, then drizzle it over the salad and add a bit more oil.

Potato Salad

SERVES 8–10
2 small red onions, peeled
4 tbsp red wine vinegar
pinch of caster sugar
1.2kg new potatoes,
    scrubbed
6 spring onions,
    finely chopped
salt

Dressing
130ml sunflower oil
40ml Safari brown vinegar
    (or other brown vinegar)
3 tbsp sugar
1 tsp black pepper
1 tsp garlic salt
½ tsp table salt
2 tbsp crème fraîche
4 tbsp mayonnaise

This is great with chopped herring (see page 40) or makes a lovely summer salad to serve with cold meat and bread. It's simple to make but the key thing is to toss the potatoes with the dressing while they are hot. Safari brown vinegar is a distilled brown vinegar and a South African favourite, but you can use any kind of brown vinegar.

Slice the red onions as finely as you can and put them in a bowl with the vinegar, caster sugar and a pinch of salt. Give everything a really good mix with your hands, then leave the onions to marinate while you get on with the potatoes.

Cut any of the larger potatoes in half, then put them all in a large saucepan with a good pinch of salt. Cover the potatoes with cold water, then put the pan on the heat and bring to the boil. Simmer the potatoes for 15–20 minutes until they're tender. While the potatoes are cooking, mix the dressing ingredients in a small jug.

Drain the potatoes immediately, put them in a large bowl with 4 tablespoons of the dressing – more if you like – and toss them well so they're all nicely coated. Add the spring onions and check the seasoning.

Tip the salad into a serving bowl, then drain the red onions from their marinade and serve them alongside.

Artichoke Platter

SERVES 8–10
2 lemons
2 bay leaves
8–10 globe artichokes
large bunch of parsley
crusty bread, to serve

Dressing
250ml sunflower oil
80ml Safari brown vinegar
   (or other brown vinegar)
2 tsp pepper
2 tsp garlic salt
½ tsp table salt

Unless you have a huge pan, cook your artichokes in a couple of batches or halve the recipe. The dressing recipe is generous but it's so good – we like to make loads and serve any extra on the side for dipping the leaves.

Half fill a large saucepan with cold water. Cut the lemons in half and squeeze the juice into the water, then chuck in the squeezed halves and the bay leaves. Bring the water to the boil, then turn it down to a simmer.

Meanwhile, remove the outer layer of tough leaves from the artichokes and throw them away. Trim the sharp top leaves with a pair of scissors. Add the artichokes to the simmering water and cook them for 20–25 minutes until they're tender.

Drain the artichokes, then cut them into quarters and place them on serving platter. Mix the dressing in a small jug and drizzle about 200ml of it over the salad, then finely chop the parsley and scatter it over the top. Serve with the rest of the dressing on the side and lots of crusty bread to mop up the juices.

Nutty Butternut Salad

SERVES 8

2 large butternut squash
2 tbsp runny honey
2 tbsp sunflower oil
1 tbsp sunflower seeds
1 tbsp pumpkin seeds
   (or the seeds from
   your squash)
25g pecan nuts
25g unsalted peanuts
100g baby spinach
2 tbsp roasted salted
   giant corn
small bunch of chives,
   roughly snipped
salt and black pepper

Dressing
65ml sunflower oil
20ml Safari brown vinegar
   (or other brown vinegar)
1 tbsp sugar
½ tsp black pepper
½ tsp garlic salt
¼ tsp table salt
4 tbsp mayonnaise
4 tbsp plain yoghurt
2 tsp peanut butter

The giant corn really makes this salad, giving it crunch and texture. We saw the corn in the supermarket and wondered what it would taste like – sensational.

Preheat the oven to 200°C/Fan 180°C/Gas 6. Peel the squash and cut them into wedges. Put the wedges in a big bowl and toss them with a tablespoon of the honey and the sunflower oil, then season with salt and pepper. Tip the wedges on to a baking tray and bake them for 45 minutes until soft and slightly caramelized. Leave them to cool slightly.

Meanwhile, toast the seeds and nuts in a dry frying pan for a couple of minutes. When they begin to colour, add the remaining tablespoon of honey and a good pinch of salt. Let the nuts and seeds caramelize for 30 seconds, then take the pan off the heat and leave the nuts and seeds to cool.

Mix all the dressing ingredients together in a jug. Roughly chop the seeds and nuts, leaving the smaller ones whole. Spread the spinach on a serving dish, top with the squash, then scatter the nuts, seeds and giant corn on top. Drizzle the thick creamy dressing over the salad and scatter it with chives.

Pasta Salad

SERVES 6

2 carrots, peeled
1 cucumber, peeled
  and cut in half
300g bow-tie pasta
  (farfalle)
2 corn cobs, leaves
  stripped off
1 yellow pepper,
  deseeded and sliced
1 red pepper, deseeded
  and sliced
75g Cheddar cheese,
  crumbled
75g pine nuts, toasted
220g good-quality
  canned tuna, drained
salt

Dressing

130ml sunflower oil
40ml Safari brown vinegar
  (or other brown vinegar)
2 tbsp sugar
1 tsp black pepper
1 tsp garlic salt
½ tsp table salt

Everyone loves a pasta salad and this one is made extra good with the addition of juicy sweetcorn kernels. If you don't have corn cobs you could use a couple of handfuls of frozen corn instead.

Using a vegetable peeler, cut the carrots and cucumber into long ribbons and put them in a large salad bowl.

Bring a big saucepan of water to the boil and add a good pinch of salt. Add the pasta and boil for 9–10 minutes, or according to the directions on the packet, until it's perfectly cooked. Pop the corn cobs into the pan for the final 5 minutes. Drain the pasta and remove the corn cobs.

Slice the kernels off the corn cobs and put them in a large bowl with the pasta and the rest of the ingredients. Mix the dressing and add it to the salad, then toss well and serve.

Mom's Fiat 500

✳·✳

Once mom got an idea in her head there was absolutely no stopping her. One day she saw something about taxi drivers in India who decorated their cabs beautifully and that was that. She was going to get an old car and cover it with beading and other embellishments.

We found a Fiat 500 for sale – it didn't even have a gearbox. The guy who sold it to us left it down the street and we had to push it home. Huffing and puffing, we shoved it down the side of the house and into the garden, but mom, with her artistic mastery, was not satisfied. She insisted it had to be turned round and we had to move the car again. But the position was still not right. She wanted it moved to the other side of the terrace. So the six of us attempted to move the car, again! It was a little car but it was heavy.

Then Rocky came along. Our saviour was a builder, a big man, and he had the strength of ten. He held the car up by two wheels, moved it all by himself to where mom wanted and plonked it down. It hasn't budged since and probably never will, as it has started to disintegrate and rust, which only adds to its charm.

Mom did start the beading, but before she could get very far, all the kids began playing in the car. I think mom took great joy from the fun we had, and she was more than happy to discard her art project in favour of our entertainment.

This car has chugged its way through our lives and is still a focal point at our parties and celebrations. We continue to fill the boot and bonnet with flowers, balloons and even lanterns. Mom never expected the Fiat to become what it has for us. But she had a way of knowing that there was something special in everything, even a little old car with no engine.

Funnily enough, our parents' first car was a Fiat just like this one. They bought it when they were first together.

Curried Rice Salad

250g mixed wild, brown
and basmati rice

2–3 red peppers,
deseeded and diced

410g can of apricots,
drained and diced

6 spring onions,
finely sliced

5 tbsp salad cream

5 tbsp plain yoghurt

1 tbsp medium curry
powder

salt and black pepper

Our dad loves curry and that was how this salad came about. Mom found that adding a touch of spice was a great way to spruce up a quick lunch dish. If you want to make this dish dairy-free, replace the yoghurt with some extra salad cream.

Cook the various types of rice according to the packet instructions for each – you'll probably have to cook them separately since they will have different cooking times. Drain the cooked rice in a sieve and run it all under cold water to cool.

Toss the red peppers, apricots and spring onions with the rice. Mix the salad cream with the yoghurt and curry powder, and stir it into the rice and vegetables. Season to taste, then spoon everything on to a serving plate.

Tabbouleh

SERVES 6

140g flatleaf parsley
25g mint (optional)
170g bulgur wheat
2 tomatoes, finely chopped
1 bunch spring onions,
    finely chopped, or
    1 very small white
    onion, peeled and
    finely chopped
freshly squeezed juice
    of 3 lemons
6 tbsp extra virgin olive oil
salt and black pepper

Mom was always willing to pitch up and help anyone, anywhere. One time we were all at a Bar Mitzvah in Israel. There were about 60 of us staying at the hotel and everyone was wanting their lunch. The staff was struggling to manage, so what did mom do? She knew exactly how to solve this problem so she went into the kitchen, rolled up her sleeves and got stuck in. Everyone enjoyed the food. Compliments to the chef – our mom.

First, finely chop the herbs. You might be tempted to use a food processor for this quantity, but it's far better to do it by hand. Using the machine can make the herbs go all soggy and watery.

Rinse the bulgur wheat under cold running water, then put it in a bowl of cold water to soak for 30 minutes. When the wheat has softened, drain it, then squeeze it with your hands over a sieve in the sink to get rid of as much water as possible. Put the bulgur in a serving bowl.

Add the tomatoes, chopped parsley and mint (if using) and the spring onions or onion to the bowl, then the lemon juice and olive oil. Season the salad well and leave it for 15–20 minutes for the flavours to develop. Check the seasoning before serving and add more salt and pepper if you like.

Shally's Cabbage Salad

2 x 100g packs of
 super noodles
5 tbsp sesame seeds
4 tbsp sunflower seeds
100g flaked almonds
1 large white cabbage
8 spring onions

Dressing
130ml sunflower oil
40ml Safari brown vinegar
 (or other brown vinegar)
2 tbsp sugar
1 tsp black pepper
1 tsp garlic salt
½ tsp table salt
2 tbsp ground allspice

Super noodles are instant dried noodles. They're normally added to boiling water with the flavouring sachet but for this recipe they're used just as they are. People don't believe they can work but they really do and they add a lovely crisp, crunchy texture.

Preheat the oven to 200°C/Fan 180°C/Gas 6. Remove the packet of flavouring from the noodles and chuck it away. Break the noodles up into small bite-sized pieces and lay them on a baking tray. Add the seeds and almonds and toast them all in the oven for 5–10 minutes, tossing them once. Watch them carefully – they burn very easily.

Meanwhile, wash the cabbage and slice it very finely with a sharp knife or using the shredder attachment on a food processor. Finely slice the spring onions and toss them with the cabbage, then pile everything on to a serving dish. Scatter the toasted noodles and seeds on top.

Whisk the dressing ingredients in a bowl or jug until well mixed. Pour the dressing over the salad and serve it at once.

Mixed Bean Salad

SERVES 6–8

250g green beans,
    tops trimmed
400g can of red
    kidney beans,
    drained and rinsed
400g can of butter beans,
    drained and rinsed
1 medium red onion,
    finely chopped
200g can of baked beans
salt and black pepper

Dressing

65ml sunflower oil
20ml Safari brown vinegar
    (or other brown vinegar)
1 tbsp sugar
½ tsp black pepper
½ tsp garlic salt
¼ tsp table salt

This is a really quick and easy recipe and you can make it even speedier by using canned green beans if you like. And it's very easy to add to – if more guests arrive, just open another can of beans.

Bring a pan of water to the boil, add a pinch of salt and the green beans, then simmer them for 6 minutes until just cooked. Tip them into a serving bowl.

Add the kidney beans, butter beans and red onion to the bowl, then tip in the baked beans, sauce and all. Whisk the dressing ingredients together in a small jug, then add to the salad and mix well.

Season with salt and pepper to taste and leave the salad for an hour or so before serving so the flavours have a chance to blend and develop.

Spinach & Strawberry Salad

400g strawberries, hulled
and thinly sliced
200g bag of spinach
(more if you like),
washed and drained
250g button or baby
chestnut mushrooms,
wiped clean and sliced
50g flaked almonds
25g sunflower seeds

Dressing
50g blue cheese, crumbled
or 50g Parmesan
cheese, grated
200ml soured cream
1 heaped tsp black pepper
1 heaped tsp salt
100ml mayonnaise
3 tbsp sugar
juice of 1 lemon
1 garlic clove, crushed

After a trip to Los Angeles, we noticed that mom was serving a salad on a plate that looked remarkably similar to one we'd had at our hotel. We remembered that she'd admired the fancy flower-printed plate when it arrived on a room service tray. When we asked her how she'd found something so similar in London, she replied in her usual mischievous way, "They won't miss it".

Put the strawberries and spinach leaves in a large bowl and toss them together, being careful not to damage the berries. Add the sliced mushrooms

Toast the almonds in a dry pan over a medium heat for a minute until they smell lovely and turn golden – take care not to let them burn. Leave them to cool, then add to the salad with the sunflower seeds.

Mix all the ingredients for the dressing together – blue cheese gives a good strong flavour but use Parmesan if you prefer something milder. Drizzle some dressing over the salad, then serve the rest on the side.

Papaya Salad

1 butterhead or iceberg
   lettuce, leaves separated
2 ripe papayas, peeled
   and deseeded
2 ripe avocados, peeled
   and stoned
50g hazelnuts

Dressing
65ml sunflower oil
20ml Safari brown vinegar
3 tbsp sugar
½ tsp black pepper
½ tsp garlic salt
¼ tsp table salt
4 tbsp mayonnaise
2 tsp soy sauce
½ papaya, peeled
   and deseeded

When you're making this dish, leave the avocado stone in the salad until the last minute to prevent the flesh turning brown. A squeeze of lemon over the avocado will also help.

Wash and dry the salad leaves and put them in a salad bowl or on a platter. Slice papaya and avocado flesh and add them to the leaves. Toast the hazelnuts in a dry pan, then chop them roughly and sprinkle them over the salad.

Blitz all the dressing ingredients in a food processor and pour the dressing over the salad just before serving. Or if you prefer, serve the dressing in a small jug so that everyone can help themselves.

Ninety-nine Lettuces

· ✱ · ✱ · ✱ · ✱ · ✱ · ✱ · ✱ · ✱ · ✱ · ✱ · ✱ · ✱ · ✱ · ✱ · ✱ · ✱ · ✱ ·

Shally was an enthusiastic online shopper and must have been Ocado's favourite customer. But her passion for shopping was sometimes marred by her lack of expertise with technology. On one occasion she ordered 99 packs of lettuce. Ocado didn't query this, so we received the strangest of all grocery deliveries – a punnet of strawberries, a pack of carrots, a jar of mayo and 99 lettuces!

Spelt Salad

SERVES 6–8

250g spelt
1 cucumber,
    roughly chopped
2 yellow peppers,
    deseeded and
    roughly chopped
1 red pepper, deseeded
    and roughly chopped
¼ ripe pineapple,
    roughly chopped
1 small red onion, peeled
    and roughly chopped
salt and black pepper

Dressing
130ml sunflower oil
40ml Safari brown vinegar
    (or other brown vinegar)
2 tbsp sugar
1 tsp black pepper
1 tsp garlic salt
½ tsp table salt

Spelt doesn't take long to cook but if you're really short of time you can use a pack of ready-cooked spelt. This salad looks very pretty in a glass serving bowl.

Cook the spelt according to the packet instructions – 250g of raw spelt should make about 500g cooked. Leave the spelt to cool.

When the spelt has cooled, put it in a bowl with the cucumber, peppers, pineapple and red onion. Make the dressing, then add it to the salad and toss well. Season with salt and pepper. Serve the salad in a big bowl or on a platter so everyone can help themselves.

Sushi Salad

SERVES 6–8
500g sushi rice
100ml rice vinegar
2 tbsp caster sugar
2 medium carrots
1 red pepper
1 large firm avocado
juice of 1 lime
1 large cucumber
500g fresh sashimi-grade
   tuna or Atlantic salmon
   or both, thinly sliced

Dressing
2 tbsp runny honey
4 tbsp soy sauce
6 tbsp rice vinegar
2 tbsp mirin rice wine
juice of 2 or 3 limes
3 tbsp sesame oil
3 tbsp sunflower oil

To serve
wasabi mayonnaise
extra soy sauce
pickled ginger

The fish in this salad is eaten raw, Japanese style, so it must be really fresh and very good quality. Use salmon, tuna, sea bass – whatever you like – and make sure you keep it in the fridge until the very last moment. Smoked salmon also works well in this salad.

Wash the rice thoroughly until the water runs clear – it's best to do this in a sieve under a running cold tap so you can see the water coming through. Put the rice in a saucepan and cover it with cold water – there should be about a centimetre of water above the surface of the rice. Put the lid on the pan, bring the water to the boil and simmer for 15 minutes. Remove the pan from the heat, but keep the lid on and leave the rice to steam for 10 minutes.

Stir the vinegar and sugar together with a pinch of salt, then mix this into the rice. Tip the rice out on to a baking tray to cool quickly, forking it through every now and again to keep grains separate. Leave it aside while you prepare the rest of the salad ingredients.

Peel the carrots and cut them into fine ribbons with a vegetable peeler. Finely dice the red pepper, then dice the avocado flesh and sprinkle it with the lime juice. Cut the cucumber in half across the middle and dice one half finely. Pull a fork down the sides of the remaining half to remove stripes of peel, then cut the cucumber into thin slices.

Whisk all the ingredients for the dressing together in a jug or bowl.

Put the thinly sliced fish and bowls of carrots, pepper, avocado and cucumber on the table so that people can take what they want. Serve some wasabi, extra soy sauce and pickled ginger as well and use chopsticks, of course!

Onion Rings

SERVES 6
vegetable oil
3 large onions, peeled
250ml whole milk
100g plain flour
salt and black pepper

Onion rings are a classic in our home and we make them all the time. They're always so popular that people would eat them all before we had a chance to put them on the table and we'd have to quickly cook up some more. The key to success is simple – have the oil nice and hot.

Take a large saucepan and fill it about one-third full with vegetable oil. Heat the oil to 180°C, or until a breadcrumb dropped into the oil burns brown in 30 seconds. Always take great care around a pan of hot oil and never leave it unattended for a second.

Slice the onions into rounds about 0.5–1cm thick, then push all the layers out of each sliced ring to make lots of individual rings. Put these in a bowl and add the milk. Put the flour on a shallow plate and season it with salt and pepper, then remove some rings from the milk and toss them in the flour until coated.

Line a large plate with kitchen towel. Once the oil is hot enough, add a handful of rings – don't add too many, as they will just stick together and won't crisp up properly. Fry the onion rings for a couple of minutes, turning them once, until they're golden brown and crisp. Remove them with a slotted spoon and put them on the prepared plate.

Allow the oil to come back up to temperature before frying the rest of the onion rings in batches. Sprinkle them with sea salt and eat them immediately while they're beautifully crisp and hot.

Never Give Up

• * •

Mom was one of those larger-than life-characters. She became a part of everyone's lives, never shy to share a piece of her mind, and she handed out advice by the bucket load. Her laughter was something that filled the house and the sound of her feet tapping to the beat of music was something to which we all became accustomed. Throughout my life, my mom was my rock.

Despite a lack of encouragement from medical professionals regarding a delay in my speech development, my parents refused to accept any negative opinions and approached the situation in their own way. As always, they worked as a team and my mom took matters into her own hands. This was no easy feat 30 years ago. The therapies and research available then were not nearly as advanced as they are now.

Mom taught me so much of what I know today: how to communicate, how to love, how to have hope and, most significantly, how to never give up on anything.

I know my mom would burst with pride to know that I will shortly qualify as a chartered accountant and that I am on the verge of getting married to Sophie, who, ironically, thinks I talk too much! I know that in our home, Sophie and I will endeavour to build our own social kitchen together.

Significantly, for me, the launch of this book coincides with the week of my wedding. For me, this is a time when my mom will be even more present and alive in my mind.

I live each day with her motto – live, love, laugh – in mind, and I hope to continue to make her proud.

Ryan

Hot Courgettes & Potatoes

SERVES 6

1 large onion, peeled
2 large waxy potatoes,
    peeled
3 medium courgettes
1 bay leaf
1 or 2 cloves
½ tsp turmeric
½ tsp celery salt
½ tsp garlic salt
salt

Timing isn't crucial to this dish, so it's easy to do for lots of people. You can even prepare it earlier in the day, then heat it up when you're ready.

Bring a large saucepan of salted water to the boil. Chop the onion, potatoes and courgettes into 1cm pieces, then add them to the boiling water and simmer them for 10 minutes until soft.

Pound the bay leaf, cloves, turmeric, celery salt and garlic salt to a powder in a pestle and mortar.

When the vegetables are done, drain them, return them to the pan and toss with a teaspoon of the seasoning – save the rest for another time. Keep the pan on the heat for a few more minutes until the vegetables start to break up and turn a little mushy. Serve hot.

Roast Potatoes

SERVES 6

1.4kg Maris Piper
    potatoes, peeled
sunflower oil
2 tsp paprika
salt and black pepper

**These are so good that you can never have enough.
Make more than you think you'll need and they will all go.**

Preheat the oven to 200°C/Fan 180°C/Gas 6. Cut the
potatoes into quarters and put them in a large saucepan
of water. Add a good pinch of salt. Bring the water to the
boil and cook the potatoes for 3 minutes, then drain them
and tip them back into the pan to steam dry. Put the lid
back on the pan and give the potatoes a good shake to
fluff up the edges, as these are the bits that get really
lovely and crispy.

Tip the potatoes on to a large roasting tray and drizzle
them with a good glug of the oil. Add the paprika and
plenty of salt and pepper, then toss well so every potato
is coated and in oil and seasoning. Roast the potatoes
for 1 hour until they are golden and crispy on the outside.

A Serious Celebration

✳·✳

Mom's 50th was such a milestone. Fifty always is, but it was much more so for her because we were so afraid she wouldn't live to see it. She decided to have a ladies' tea with 50 of her friends. We had a little marquee in the garden with two lovely long tables. Mom was adamant that she wanted the tables laid with odd cups, saucers and plates – all mismatched – and she spent weeks looking for exactly what she wanted.

It was the most amazing day. It was meant to be a tea party, but people stayed and stayed. Husbands arrived to collect their wives and joined in. Word got around and other friends arrived so in the end we had about 300 people there. We'd hired a singer to perform for 90 minutes but he was having such a good time he stayed for eight hours. Somehow or other we produced more food during the evening – we got takeaways at some point and we made massive plates of ice cream and dessert. Not sure how, but it happened.

There's a strange thing about our family parties. The weather is always great. It can be pouring for days before and days after but on our day the sun shines. This happened on mom's birthday. The sun shone for her that day and now I'm sure she makes it shine for us.

Hasselback Potatoes

SERVES 6–8

1.5kg fairly large
   new potatoes
50g butter
2 tsp Osem onion
   soup powder
   or bouillon

This is a Swedish dish and it's a sort of mixture between roast and baked potatoes. The outsides are beautifully crispy while the insides are creamy and soft.

Preheat the oven to 200°C/Fan 180°C/Gas 6. Take a potato and slice down into it at 2mm intervals, being very careful not to cut right the way through. The potato should still be joined together at the bottom. Repeat with the remaining potatoes and place them all in a baking tray.

Melt the butter in a small pan, then pour it over the potatoes, making sure they are all well covered. Sprinkle over the soup powder or bouillon, then bake the potatoes for 40 minutes. Turn the dish halfway through so the potatoes cook evenly.

The Mains

Soy Salmon

SERVES 6–8

115ml light soy sauce,
    plus extra to serve
3 tbsp date syrup or
    golden syrup
100g granulated sugar
4 tbsp good-quality
    vegetable oil
zest and juice of 4 lemons
1 side of salmon
    (about 1kg)
100g sesame seeds
4 spring onions,
    finely sliced
salt and black pepper

This is a great dish for a party, as you can cook it earlier in the day and serve it hot, cold or at room temperature.

Put the soy sauce, syrup, sugar and oil into a roasting tin or a baking tray big enough to hold the salmon. Stir in the lemon zest and mix well, then add the side of salmon. Get your hands in there and rub the sticky marinade all over the fish so every inch is covered. Leave the fish, skin-side up, in the marinade for at least 2 hours or overnight in the fridge.

Preheat the oven to 200°C/Fan 180°C/Gas 6. Turn the salmon skin-side down and pour the lemon juice over it. Scatter the sesame seeds and half the spring onions on top and season well with salt and pepper.

Bake the salmon in the hot oven for 20–25 minutes until just done. Serve hot or cold with the remaining spring onions and a drizzle of extra soy sauce.

Crispy Baked Cod

SERVES 6

50g unsalted butter
small bunch of parsley
150g breadcrumbs
    (made from stale bread)
1 lemon
6 generous pieces of white
    fish fillet, such as cod
    or haddock
olive oil
salt and black pepper

This is such an easy way of cooking fish. You can get it all ready in advance, then pop it in the oven when you're nearly ready to eat. No stress.

Preheat the oven to 200°C/Fan 180°C/Gas 6. Melt the butter in a small saucepan, season it with salt and pepper and take the pan off the heat. Finely chop the parsley and mix it with the breadcrumbs in a bowl, then grate in the zest of the lemon. Season well.

Dip each piece of fish in the melted butter, place it in a baking tray, then top it with lemony breadcrumbs.

Finely slice the lemon and place the slices around the pieces of fish. Drizzle with olive oil and bake the fish for about 15 minutes until golden brown and just cooked.

Megan's Tuna Bake

SERVES 6

500g penne pasta
4 cans of good-quality
    tuna in olive oil
1 onion, peeled and
    finely chopped
2 garlic cloves, peeled
    and crushed
1 sprig of rosemary, leaves
    picked from the stems
    and chopped
1 sprig of thyme, leaves
    picked from the stems
    and chopped
400g can of cream
    of tomato soup
salt and black pepper

Cottage cheese topping
50g Cheddar cheese,
    coarsely grated
300g cottage cheese
150g crème fraîche

"This is my very favourite supper and the only time I ever eat fish. We used to make loads of it and freeze some in those little foil dishes for our own ready meals." (Megan)

Bring a saucepan of water to the boil, add salt and the pasta and cook the pasta for 9 minutes. Drain the pasta and set it aside.

Meanwhile, heat 2 tablespoons of oil from the cans of tuna in a pan over a medium heat. Add the onion and garlic, then the chopped herbs and sauté for 8–10 minutes until the onion is soft and translucent.

Drain the remaining oil from the cans of tuna, add the tuna to the pan with the onions and give everything a good stir. Pour in the tomato soup and let it all bubble nicely for 10 minutes. Season with plenty of pepper. Preheat the oven to 200°C/Fan 180°C/Gas 6.

Mix half the Cheddar with the cottage cheese and crème fraîche, then season to taste.

Tip the pasta into an ovenproof dish, stir half the tuna mixture into the pasta, then dollop the rest on top. Spoon the cottage cheese mix over the tuna, then sprinkle the rest of the grated Cheddar on top. Season with lots of pepper. Put the dish in the oven and bake for 30 minutes until it's all bubbling and golden.

A Natural Cook

* *

Mom was a natural in the kitchen, an instinctive and creative cook. She had loads of cookbooks but she used them as inspiration, rather than following the recipes. She'd look at a picture of something and then do it her own way to get the taste she liked. Of course, her way meant making the dish to feed crowds of people.

Shally couldn't do just one guest. There were always lots of people for Friday night dinner and she always made far too much food. People would go to their own Friday night dinners and then come to us and have more. Food was the way mom drew people in and showed her love.

And when people were leaving she would always whip out the foil and say, "What do you want to take home?" She'd give them all the leftovers – and then be ready to start planning another delicious meal.

Curried Fish

SERVES 6

1kg cod or haddock loin
2 tbsp olive oil
2 medium onions, peeled
    and finely sliced
3 bay leaves
1 tsp green peppercorns
300ml white wine vinegar
250g dried apricots
100g chutney
50g apricot or peach jam
2 tsp cornflour
3 tsp curry powder
salt and black pepper

For a cheat's version, you can make this dish using fried fish from a fish and chip shop or fish balls – those little balls of minced fish. Both are delicious. As the fish is already cooked, all you need to do is make the sauce, mix it with the fish and warm it through in the oven.

Preheat the oven to 200°C/Fan 180°C/Gas 6. Cut the fish into 6 portions and season them well. Put the fish in a baking dish, drizzle it with a tablespoon of the oil, then bake in the hot oven for 10 minutes or until just cooked through.

Meanwhile, heat the remaining oil in a frying pan and add the onions, bay leaves and green peppercorns. Fry them over a high heat for a couple of minutes until the onions have slightly caramelized and softened, then pour in 250ml of water. Bring the water to a boil and simmer for 5 minutes, or until all the water has gone. Tip the onions out of the pan and set them aside.

Pour the vinegar into the pan and add 300ml of water, the apricots, chutney and jam. Let everything bubble over a medium heat for 5 minutes until the apricots plump up. In a small bowl, mix the cornflour and curry powder with a little water to form a loose paste, then add this to the apricot sauce. Stir until thickened, then set aside to cool slightly.

When the fish is ready, put it on a serving dish and scatter with the onions. Pour the sauce over the top and you're ready to go.

Nutty Parmesan Sole

SERVES 6

100g unsalted butter,
    at room temperature
50g Parmesan cheese,
    finely grated
12 lemon sole fillets,
    pin-boned and skin on
100g flaked almonds
    (or chopped whole
    almonds)
2 lemon wedges
salt and black pepper

This works well with any white fish but is particularly good with lemon sole. It's another of those lovely recipes you can prepare in advance, all ready to pop in the oven when people want to eat.

Preheat the oven to 200°C/Fan 180°C/Gas 6. You will need a couple of large shallow baking dishes. Spread about 25g of the butter over the base of each dish. Sprinkle about one-quarter of the cheese into each dish over the butter.

Place about 6 sole fillets in each dish, skin-side down. Season them with salt and pepper, then dot with the remaining butter. Mix the almonds with the remaining cheese and sprinkle over the top.

Bake the fish in the oven for 10–14 minutes, until it's beautifully golden and perfectly cooked. Serve drizzled with the buttery pan juices and garnish with lemon wedges. Nice with some greens and boiled new potatoes.

Mushroom Risotto

SERVES 6

30g dried porcini
 mushrooms
1 chicken stock cube
1 tbsp olive oil
30g butter
1 medium white onion,
 peeled and finely
 chopped
400g risotto rice
100g of wild mushrooms
50g Parmesan cheese,
 grated
handful of chopped
 parsley (optional)
salt and black pepper

This is a perfect dish to rustle up at a moment's notice because you'll have most of the ingredients in your cupboard. You don't have to use wild mushrooms – any sort will do.

Break up the dried mushrooms and put them in a bowl. Bring a pan with 1.5 litres of water to the boil and crumble in the stock cube. Ladle a little of the stock over the mushrooms and leave them to soak. Leave the stock to simmer gently over a low heat.

Put the oil and one-third of the butter in a separate pan. Once the butter has melted and is sizzling, add the chopped onion and cook for 8–10 minutes until it's all softened and translucent. Add the rice and toss to coat in the oil and butter, then add the dried mushrooms and their soaking water. Start to add the simmering stock a ladleful at a time, stirring well and letting it all be absorbed before adding the next. Continue until you've used all the liquid and the rice is cooked but still al dente. This will take 20–25 minutes.

Take the pan off the heat and add another third of the butter and half the Parmesan. Put the lid on the pan and leave the risotto to stand for a couple of minutes.

Cook the wild mushrooms in the rest of the butter. Stir the risotto and check the seasoning, adding a little salt and pepper if needed. Serve the risotto garnished with the mushrooms, the rest of the grated Parmesan and some parsley if you like.

Ryan's Chicken Schnitzels

SERVES 4

4 medium chicken breasts
100g matzo meal
1 tsp garlic salt
2 tsp paprika
4 eggs
vegetable oil
lemon wedges, to serve

"One of the first dishes my mom ever taught me to cook was chicken schnitzels and I've always loved them. It took me a while to master the technique of coating the chicken pieces, but I managed it, and I still cook these for my friends." (Ryan)

Lay out a large piece of cling film on your work surface. Put the chicken breasts on top, leaving quite a bit of space between them, then cover them with another sheet of cling film. Take a rolling pin and give the chicken a really good bashing until all the breasts are flattened and about 5mm thick – this is a great way to take out all the frustrations of the day!

Mix the matzo meal with the garlic salt and paprika and spread it out on a plate. Crack the eggs into a wide shallow bowl and beat them well. Dip each chicken breast into the egg mixture, then into the matzo meal, pressing them down on each side to make sure they are well covered.

Heat a good glug of oil in a large frying pan over a medium heat. Add a couple of the schnitzels and cook them for 2–3 minutes on each side until completely golden and cooked through. Carefully lift them out and place them on some kitchen towel to drain while you cook the others.

Serve with lemon wedges to squeeze over the chicken and a green salad.

Pot-roast Chicken

SERVES 6
olive oil
12 shallots, peeled
8 carrots, peeled
   and chopped into
   3cm chunks
1 garlic bulb, cut in half
1 large free-range chicken
3 sprigs of thyme
glass of white wine
400g Maris Piper potatoes,
   peeled and quartered
juice of ½ lemon
salt and black pepper

There's nothing so cosy and comforting as a pot-roast chicken, shared with family and friends. And it's all cooked in one pot so there's not much washing up.

Preheat the oven to 200°C/Fan 180°C/Gas 6. Heat a little olive oil in a large flameproof casserole dish and add the shallots. Cook the shallots gently for 5 minutes over a medium heat until they're beginning to caramelize, then add the carrots and garlic. Cook for another 5 minutes, remove all the vegetables with a slotted spoon and set them aside on a plate.

Heat a little more oil in the casserole dish. Season the chicken all over, then add it to the casserole and brown it on all sides until it's beautifully golden.

Put the vegetables back in the casserole and add the thyme, white wine and a large glass of water (about 200ml). Season again, then put the lid on the casserole and place it in the oven. Cook for 45 minutes, then remove the casserole dish from the oven, baste the chicken with the juices and add the potatoes. Pop it back into the oven and cook for another 45 minutes. Squeeze some lemon juice over the chicken before serving. Some seasonal greens make a good side dish for this.

Chutney Chicken

SERVES 6

250ml ketchup
250ml onion chutney
    (Mrs Ball's is best)
250ml brown sauce
2 tbsp soy sauce
2 tbsp Worcestershire
    sauce
6 chicken thighs and
    6 chicken drumsticks,
    skin on and bone in

The chutney is all important in this dish. Any onion chutney is fine but our family favourite is Mrs Ball's onion chutney, original flavour. It's one of the best known of all South African products.

Preheat the oven to 200°C/Fan 180°C/Gas 6. Mix all the ingredients, except the chicken, together in a bowl or jug. You can do this well ahead if you like and keep the sauce mixture in the fridge.

Toss the chicken pieces in the sauce and then put them in a baking dish. Cook the chicken in the hot oven for 1 hour, basting every 20 minutes. Remove the chicken from the oven and, using a metal spoon, skim off as much fat from the surface as you can. Serve with a salad.

Sweet & Sticky Chicken

SERVES 6

6 whole chicken legs
6 tbsp salad cream
1 tbsp Dijon mustard
1 tbsp Worcestershire
 sauce
6 tbsp mango chutney
salt and black pepper

People think this takes ages to make but it is so easy, you wouldn't believe. And it tastes amazing. Everyone loves it.

Preheat the oven to 200°C/Fan 180°C/Gas 6. Using a sharp knife, cut deep slashes in each chicken leg, then put them all in a large baking tray or a roasting tin.

Mix the remaining ingredients and season with salt and pepper, then pour half the mixture over the chicken and rub it into each leg. Really get in there with your hands and massage the mixture in lovingly.

Bake the chicken in the hot oven for 50 minutes until it's all bubbling and golden. Pour the rest of the sauce over the chicken and cook for another 10 minutes, then take the dish out of the oven. Skim off as much fat as you can and serve the chicken with a salad and some crusty bread.

Thankfully, She Chose Me

* *

As it happened, my paternal grandmother knew Shally's maternal grandmother. They were distantly related. So when Shally started at the same hotel school as me I was told to look out for her.

I asked her out on a date and although she was going out with someone else at the time she said yes. I drove from Benoni, which is about 45 minutes, to fetch her and we went into the centre of Johannesburg to see a movie. I remember it was called *I Love My Wife*. As we got in the lift at the cinema complex I said: "I'm going to marry you". Shally was not impressed! But, luckily for me, six months later she changed her mind.

Shally was a smoker. When we first came to the UK we lived in a tiny bedsit and she smoked 80 cigarettes a day. I would come home and everything stank of smoke. One night I told her I couldn't take it any more and she would have to choose – cigarettes or me. She chose cigarettes and I left.

I sat outside on my suitcase and waited. Half an hour later she joined me on the curb and she gave up the cigs. (Lawrence)

Lawrence & Shally

👉 *we cater for all functions from biscuits to banquets.*

Barmen & Waiters Etc., Also Available.

Phone 784-3442
or 54-2049
or 54-9105

That's Love

* *

My sister had graduated from the University of Southern California in LA and we were all set to go to the ceremony. Sadly, mom wasn't well enough to come along and my dad didn't want to leave her, so my brother and I and my best friend had to go without them.

Happily, dad decided to fly out to join us at the last moment. When he arrived, we spotted a Tommy Hilfigger label stitched to the front of his shirt by his belly button. When we'd stopped laughing we asked him what was going on.

He explained that just before he was due to leave for the airport mom had noticed a hole in his shirt. Dad would have changed and chucked it out, but mom liked the shirt – and hated waste – so ordered him to take it off. She immediately unpicked the label, stitched it over the hole in the front and gave it back – good to go.

He wore it, of course! Why not? It kept Shally with him when he was thousands of miles away and reminded him of her love. He still has the shirt. (Dani)

Classic Roast Chicken & Gravy

SERVES 6

1 free-range chicken
  (about 2kg or so)
1 lemon
1 tsp garlic salt
1 tsp paprika
olive oil
small bunch of thyme,
  leaves picked from
  the stems
1 tbsp flour
500ml chicken stock
  (or water from cooking
  vegetables)
salt and black pepper

For our family this is the go-to Friday night dish. We would always cook two or more chickens, as extra people would always appear during the evening.

Preheat the oven to 200°C/Fan 180°C/Gas 6.

Put the chicken in a roasting tin. Cut the lemon in half squeeze the halves over the chicken and then put them in the cavity. Season the chicken with the garlic salt and paprika, then with salt and pepper. Drizzle a good glug of olive oil over the bird and scatter with the thyme leaves.

Put the roasting tin in the oven and cook the chicken for 1–1½ hours, until the juice runs clear when you pull the leg away from the body. Put the chicken on a warm serving dish, cover it and leave it to rest for a good half an hour.

To make the gravy, put the roasting tray over a low heat and whisk the flour into the delicious roasting juices. Gradually pour in the stock, whisking continuously until you have a lovely rich gravy.

Serve with seasonal greens and roast potatoes (see p.101).

Roasted Cola Chicken

SERVES 6

1 free-range chicken
250ml cola (not the
   diet version)
100ml Mrs Ball's
   classic chutney
1 tbsp onion soup powder
   (Osem is best)
2 tbsp tomato purée
2 tbsp ground ginger
bunch of watercress,
   to serve

Osem soup powder is best for this so if you don't have any don't use anything else instead – just some seasoning. The chicken needs spatchcocking for this recipe, which simply means cutting it so it can be laid flat for quick cooking or grilling.

———————————————————————————

Preheat the oven to 200°C/Fan 180°C/Gas 6. Now you need to spatchcock your chicken. Put the chicken breast-side down. Find the backbone and using a good pair of kitchen scissors or poultry shears, cut along on each side of the backbone. Keep the scissors right next to the backbone. Remove the backbone, then turn the chicken over again and press down hard to flatten it.

Place the chicken in a roasting tin. Using a sharp knife, score the chicken all over – this will allow all the flavours to soak into the flesh. Mix together the remaining ingredients in a bowl, then pour the mixture over the chicken and massage it in well with your hands.

Put the chicken in the oven for 30 minutes, then take it out and baste it with the sticky sauce in the tin. Add a splash of water to the base of the tin, then put the chicken back in the oven for another 30 minutes. Let it rest before serving with some watercress.

Cornflake Chicken

SERVES 6
6 chicken breasts
250ml Italian dressing
150g cornflakes
salt and black pepper
vegetable oil

You can make this with matzo meal crumbs, but we were always running out of them so we started to use cornflakes instead. We always had some of those in the cupboard. Other cereals, such as Special K, are yummy too. Make sure you get some of the lovely buttery crumbs at the bottom of the tray – they are so good.

Put the chicken breasts in a bowl and pour the dressing over them. Toss the chicken breasts well to make sure they are all coated in dressing, then leave them to marinate for 2–3 hours.

Preheat the oven to 200°C/Fan 180°C/Gas 6. Gently crush the cornflakes, then pour them on to a shallow plate. Taking one chicken breast at a time, coat them in the cornflakes so they are all well covered.

Place the chicken breasts on a large roasting tray, scatter any cornflakes that are left over them and then add any remaining dressing.

Season the chicken breasts and drizzle them with a little oil, then bake them in the hot oven for 30–40 minutes until they are cooked through and golden brown. Serve with a salad and some greenery.

Chicken Sosaties Kebabs

SERVES 6

2 tbsp vegetable oil
2 garlic cloves, crushed
6 tbsp curry powder
2 tbsp ground ginger
4 tbsp sugar
2 tsp allspice
60ml balsamic vinegar
5 tbsp apricot jam
3 tbsp chutney
   (we like Mrs Ball's)
1 chicken stock cube
700g chicken breast,
   cut into chunks
4 red onions, peeled
   and quartered
400g bag of dried apricots
2 red peppers, deseeded
   and cut into chunks

Sosaties is a traditional South African dish, often made with lamb. Recipes vary but usually include apricots and red peppers as well as the meat.

Heat the vegetable oil in a small saucepan and gently cook the crushed garlic. Mix the curry powder, ginger, sugar and allspice in a bowl, then add them to the pan and cook for 30 seconds. Add the vinegar, jam, chutney and 240ml of water and crumble in the stock cube. Bring to the boil and cook for about 5 minutes, then take the pan off the heat. Leave the sauce to cool.

Take 6 long skewers and thread on alternate chunks of chicken, red onion quarters, apricots and red pepper. Put them in a dish, pour the cooled sauce over the top and leave the kebabs to marinate overnight in the fridge.

Next day, remove the kebabs from the marinade and grill them on a barbecue or in a griddle pan until the chicken is cooked through.

Dinner is Served

* *

Our mom started cooking at a very young age. Her flair in the kitchen was natural and obvious. One of her favourite people to cook for was her father, our grandpa, and one night she planned to prepare a delicious stew for him. She found some meat in the freezer, then gathered vegetables, pepper, salt, tomatoes and other bits and pieces from the cupboards. She packed the stew pot and mixed the ingredients slowly and lovingly, watching her meal come to life. She set the table in her outdoor Wendy House, a perfect setting for her brothers and her dad to enjoy their food. Our grandpa loved the stew and called for seconds, which delighted mom!

The morning after this scrumptious feast, no one could find the dogs' meat in the fridge – leftover scraps that had been bought from the butcher. The meat had vanished. Only then did mom realise she had served that meat to her dad and brothers. She's probably the only person on earth who could make a dog's breakfast into a meal fit for a king.

Mustard Chicken

SERVES 4
25g butter
1 tbsp olive oil
6–8 chicken thighs,
    skinned and boned
25g plain flour
250ml chicken stock
100ml double cream
2 tbsp Dijon mustard
1 tsp honey
salt and black pepper

Although this is so quick and easy to make, it has a beautifully rich sauce that tastes really special. Lovely served with mash and some green vegetables.

Melt the butter with the oil in a large flameproof casserole dish over a medium heat. Once the fat has started to bubble, add the chicken thighs, turn up the heat and gently brown the thighs on each side for 5 minutes. Remove them from the pan with a slotted spoon and set them aside.

Whisk the flour into the fat in the pan to make a thick paste. Very slowly pour in the stock, then the cream and whisk constantly until you have a lovely thick sauce.

Add the mustard and honey, then put the chicken back in the casserole. Simmer gently for 20 minutes until the chicken is cooked through and the sauce is rich and golden. Season to taste, then enjoy.

Sweet & Spicy Roast Turkey

SERVES 8

6–7kg free-range turkey
2 large carrots
4 celery sticks
1 eating apple
1 tbsp paprika
500ml tomato juice
250ml ginger ale
pinch of garlic salt
salt and black pepper

For some reason the apple in this recipe makes all the difference. If you're just cooking a crown or pieces of turkey rather than a whole bird, you could just add the apple quarters to the other ingredients in the tin.

Take the turkey out of the fridge an hour or two before cooking to allow it get up to room temperature. Preheat the oven to 200°C/Fan 180°C/Gas 6.

Put turkey in a large, deep roasting tray. Cut the carrots and celery sticks in half and the apples into quarters and stuff them all into the cavity of the turkey.

Mix together the paprika, tomato juice, ginger ale and garlic salt in a bowl, then add a glass of water (about 200ml) and season with salt and pepper. Pour this mixture over the turkey, then put it in the oven and roast for 3 hours. Turn the turkey every 30 minutes and if some parts are cooking quicker than others, cover them with foil.

After 3 hours check to see if the turkey is done. If you have a meat thermometer, put it into the thickest part of the thigh. If the turkey is done, the thermometer should reach 80°C. Otherwise, just pierce the thigh and look at the juices. If they run clear the turkey is ready.

Take the bird out of the oven, place it on a board or serving dish and cover it with foil. Leave it to rest for an hour while you prepare all your side dishes – roast potatoes (see p.101) are a must.

When you're ready to eat, slice or shred the meat. Reheat the rich tomatoey juices and serve them with the turkey.

Shally's Bolognese Sauce

SERVES 6–8

1kg beef mince
1 white onion,
    peeled and diced
2 tbsp oil
½ tsp garlic salt
½ tsp paprika
70g double-concentrate
    tomato purée
4 tbsp tomato ketchup
2½ tbsp Mrs Ball's chutney
1 tsp Worcestershire sauce
1 chicken stock cube
2 x 400g cans of chopped
    tomatoes
¼ tsp dried oregano
600g pasta
salt and black pepper

Mom's spag bol is just right for a small family gathering, rather than a party. You'd need a pan the size of a bath to cook pasta for a big bunch of people.

Fry the meat in a large saucepan over a medium heat for about 10 minutes or until browned. Stir from time to time to break the meat up. The meat will release quite a bit of liquid as it browns so drain it into a sieve, then tip it back in the saucepan. Add the onion and oil to the pan and stir well, then add the garlic salt, paprika, tomato purée, ketchup and chutney and season with salt and pepper to taste.

Crumble the stock cube into the pan and add the tomatoes and 120ml of water – you can use the water to rinse out the cans if you like so you don't have any waste. Cook the sauce for about 20 minutes, then add the oregano.

Meanwhile cook the pasta in lots of boiling salted water according to the packet instructions. Drain the pasta and serve it with the sauce.

Cottage Pie

SERVES 6–8
1.5kg floury potatoes
Shally's Bolognese sauce
    (see p.148)
salt and black pepper

We'd always make double quantities of mom's Bolognese sauce (see page 148), eat it with pasta one night, then use the rest for a cottage pie another time. We'd also freeze some in foil dishes for our own home-made ready meals.

Peel the potatoes, cut them into chunks and put them in a large pan of salted water. Bring them to the boil and cook until tender, then mash and season with salt and pepper. Leave the mash to cool for a short while. Preheat the oven to 200°C/Fan 180°C/Gas 6.

Using a slotted spoon to drain off some of the liquid, dollop the meat sauce into a deep pie dish. Pile the mash on top, then make patterns in it with a fork. Bake in the preheated oven for 30–40 minutes or until the filling is piping hot and the topping is lovely and brown.

Slow-cooked Red Lamb Shanks

SERVES 4

4 garlic cloves, peeled
2 sprigs of rosemary, leaves
  picked from the stems
2 tbsp olive oil
4 large lamb shanks
2 onions, peeled and sliced
2 carrots, peeled and
  roughly chopped
400g can of tomatoes
125ml tomato ketchup
1 tsp smoked paprika
1 tsp ground ginger
3 tbsp Worcestershire
  sauce
2 tbsp red wine or
  Safari brown vinegar
  (or other brown vinegar)
2 tbsp golden syrup
3 tsp English mustard
  powder
2 bay leaves
salt and black pepper

These lamb shanks are cooked until the meat is falling off the bone. People used to fight over them – they are that good. Perfect served with some fluffy mash to soak up the delicious juices.

Preheat the oven to 220°C/Fan 200°C/Gas 7. Crush the garlic in a pestle and mortar, add the rosemary and oil, then some salt and pepper and pound everything to a coarse paste.

Using a sharp knife, make long slits in each shank, then rub the delicious paste all over the meat – use your hands for this and really get in there and massage the meat. Put the shanks in a casserole dish and pop them in the oven for 30 minutes to brown.

Put the onions and carrots in a bowl, add the remaining ingredients and mix everything together well. Once the lamb has had 30 minutes in the oven, take the casserole out and pour the onion and carrot mixture over the shanks. Put a lid on the dish, turn the oven down to 200°C/Fan 180°C/Gas 6 and cook the lamb for another 2 hours. Baste the meat regularly and remove the lid for the last 30 minutes so the meat can brown on top.

Minty Roast Leg of Lamb

SERVES 6–8

small bunch of mint,
    leaves picked from
    the stems
6 tbsp mint jelly
2 tsp sweet smoked paprika
2 tbsp olive oil
1 large orange, cut in half
2kg leg of lamb
salt and black pepper

A classic combo of lamb and mint, this is a simple classic and so good. You can also make it with racks of lamb if you like and serve it with more mint jelly or mint sauce.

Preheat the oven to 220°C/Fan 200°C/Gas 7. Mix together the mint leaves, mint jelly, smoked paprika, olive oil and the juice of the orange in a small jug. Cut deep slits into the lamb, then rub the mix all over the meat with your hands. Give the lamb a good massage, making sure you get the mixture into the slits. Season the joint well, then put it in a roasting tin. Add a glass of water (about 200ml) to the tin and pop in the squeezed orange halves as well.

Roast the lamb for 1 hour and 15 minutes for slightly pink meat, or 1 hour and 30 minutes for well done. If the lamb starts to brown too much, cover it with foil halfway through the cooking time and add a little more water to the roasting tin to stop the juices burning.

When the meat is cooked to your liking, remove it from the oven, put it on a board and leave it to rest for 15–30 minutes before carving. Put the roasting tin on the hob, add a tablespoon of cornflour to thicken the juices and make a delicious gravy. Serve with hasselback potatoes (see p.106) and green vegetables.

Mom's Scrapbooks

·*·

Mom adored making scrapbooks. And as with everything she did, these scrapbooks were extraordinary. They were filled with an array of anything she found along the way – a good joke, a memorable business card, the fortune from her Chinese cookie, colourful sweet wrappers, swatches of fabric – and of course, an ever-growing, never-ending collection of old and new recipes. My mother would save all these treasures of inspiration in small vintage suitcases that piled up under the table in her studio.

Every now and then she would go through the cases and create her scrapbooks. Each and every one of the pieces that filled these suitcases was thoughtfully placed on a page to inspire a creative process.

These books are an expression of her unlimited talent and her ability to visualize the endless possibilities in even in the smallest of scraps.

Custard.

Boil 2½ cups milk and meantime
beat 2 eggs, ½ cup sugar 1 heaped
teaspoon maizena, 2 table spoons flour
together in a little milk and when milk boils
add this beaten mixture to
milk and boil till done. Just
before taking off add 1 table spoon
butter & 1 teasp vanilla essence.

Pick-&-Mix Burgers

SERVES 8

1kg good-quality
   beef mince
1 medium onion, peeled
   and finely chopped
handful of parsley,
   finely chopped
1 medium egg
2 tbsp olive oil
salt and black pepper

Quick pickled cucumbers

1 cucumber
3 tbsp white wine vinegar
1 tbsp caster sugar

To serve

onion rings (see p.96)
2 beef tomatoes, sliced
1 pineapple, peeled
   and sliced
avocado
lettuce
8 burger buns

This is a great family favourite. Everyone always loves choosing their fillings and making their own burger. It gets people talking and makes for a really fun meal.

First prepare the cucumbers. Using the prongs of a fork, scrape down the length of the cucumber to remove stripes of peel. Finely slice the cucumber. Mix the vinegar with the sugar and a pinch of salt in a bowl, then add the cucumber slices and mix everything together with your hands. All the slices should be well covered with the vinegar mixture. Leave for 30 minutes before serving.

For the burgers, put the mince in a bowl, add the onion, parsley, egg and a good seasoning of salt and pepper and mix well. Shape the mixture into 8 burgers and rub them all over in oil.

Heat a large non-stick frying pan over a high heat and cook the burgers for 3–4 minutes on each side or until just done. (These are also good cooked on a barbecue.)

Put the pickled cucumbers, onion rings, tomato, pineapple, avocado and lettuce on the table with the buns and let everyone pick their fillings and build their burger.

Sweet & Sour Meatballs

SERVES 6

1kg beef mince
1 onion, peeled and
  coarsely grated
1 small potato, peeled
  and coarsely grated
50g fine matzo meal
salt and black pepper

Sweet and sour sauce

1 large onion, peeled
  and finely sliced
2 tbsp golden syrup
2 heaped tbsp
  long-grain rice
2 tbsp tomato purée
juice of 1 lemon
1 tsp ground cinnamon

These yummy sticky meatballs practically fall apart in your mouth. So delicious.

Put the beef, onion, potato and matzo meal in a bowl, mix it all well and season generously with salt and pepper. Shape the mixture into balls about the size of golf balls. Put them in the fridge to firm up until needed.

For the sauce, place a high-sided frying pan or casserole dish over a medium heat and add the sliced onion and golden syrup. Turn the heat to low and cook the onion slowly for 20 minutes, stirring constantly, until it's all softened and caramelized.

Add 500ml water to the pan and bring it to the boil. Add the rice, tomato purée, lemon juice, cinnamon and meatballs and season again. Put the lid on the pan and leave it all to cook for about an hour. The sauce should be thick and rich by this time. Serve in bowls with rice.

Onion Beef

SERVES 8–10

splash of oil
2kg beef brisket
   in one piece
3 large onions, peeled
   and finely sliced
4 large Portobello
   mushrooms, finely sliced
2 garlic cloves, peeled
   and finely chopped
2 sprigs of thyme
2 tbsp Worcestershire
   sauce
2 tbsp light soy sauce
2 tbsp onion chutney
1 tbsp Osem onion
   soup powder
30g pickled silverskin
   onions, drained
750ml beef stock

The brisket will look like a big piece of meat, but you'll be surprised how much it shrinks as it cooks. The onion soup powder adds seasoning so if you don't have any, add salt and pepper to taste.

Preheat the oven to 200°C/Fan 180°C/Gas 6. Add the oil to a wide flameproof casserole dish and place it over a high heat. Add the brisket – no need for seasoning as the soup powder has seasoning – and sear it for 5 minutes on each side until it's golden brown all over.

Take the beef out of the pan and put it on a board or plate. Add the onions, mushrooms, garlic and thyme to the pan and cook them briefly in the meat juices, then add all the other ingredients.

Pop the beef back in the pan, put it in the oven and cook, uncovered, for 1½ hours. Keep an eye on the sauce and if it starts to look too thick, add more water. At the end of the 1½ hours, put the lid on the pan or cover it tightly with foil and continue to cook for another 2 hours, basting the meat with the sauce every half an hour or so.

By the end of the cooking time, the beef should be very tender and just about shreddable. Remove it from the oven and leave it to rest for 15 minutes.

Slice or shred the meat, then reheat the sauce and put the meat back into the pan to serve. Great with potatoes or just crusty bread and a salad to mop up the luscious juices.

Beef Stew

SERVES 6–8

3 tbsp sunflower oil
1kg beef skirt or flank
  steak, cut into
  bite-sized chunks
2 onions, peeled and
  roughly chopped
2 celery sticks,
  roughly chopped
4 medium carrots,
  peeled and chopped
2 sprigs rosemary,
  leaves picked from
  the stems and chopped
2 heaped tbsp
  tomato purée
2 x 400g cans of
  chopped tomatoes
750ml beef stock
2 tsp English
  mustard powder
6 medium potatoes,
  peeled and quartered
300g green beans,
  tops trimmed
salt and black pepper

There are potatoes in this stew, but we still like to serve some rice alongside to soak up the delicious juices.

Put a large flameproof casserole dish over a high heat and add 2 tablespoons of the oil. When the oil is hot, fry the chunks of beef for about 5 minutes or until they are lovely and brown on the outside. It's best to do this in batches so you don't overcrowd the dish, or the meat will steam and not brown. Take out each batch of meat as it browns and put it on a plate.

When all the beef is browned, add the onions, celery, carrots and rosemary to the casserole. Tip all the browned beef back in as well, turn down the heat and add the rest of the oil. Cook everything gently for about 8 minutes, then add the tomato purée, tomatoes, beef stock and mustard powder. Turn up the heat and bring the stew to the boil. Pop a lid on the casserole dish, reduce the heat and leave the stew to simmer for 1 hour, stirring occasionally.

Add the potatoes to the casserole and continue to cook for another 30–45 minutes, adding the green beans for the last 10–15 minutes of the cooking time.

By this time the beef should be beautifully tender. Take the casserole off the heat and season the stew with salt and pepper until it tastes the way you like it. Supper is good to go – perhaps with some rice and a green salad.

Ginger Ale Brisket

SERVES 8–10

3 large onions,
   peeled and chopped
   into wedges
1 litre ginger ale
1 tbsp Osem onion
   soup powder
4 tbsp tomato ketchup
2 tsp black peppercorns
8 bay leaves
3kg beef brisket, boned,
   rolled and tied
salt and black pepper

Don't worry – your butcher will bone, roll and tie the brisket for you and give you a lovely neat parcel to take home and cook. This has to be in the oven for hours but it's well worth the wait.

Preheat the oven to 200°C/Fan 180°C/Gas 6. Put the onion wedges in a large casserole dish and add the ginger ale, soup powder, ketchup, peppercorns and bay leaves. Season the brisket all over with plenty of salt and pepper, then put it in the casserole with 250ml just-boiled water. Turn the brisket so it's nicely coated with the sauce ingredients.

Pop the lid on the casserole dish, put it in the oven and cook for 2 hours. Remove the casserole and turn the meat, then put it back into the oven. Cook for another 2 hours until the meat is not quite falling apart but still easy to slice.

Take the beef out of the dish and put it on a board to rest. Skim off any fat from the juices, put the casserole on a high heat and cook until the gravy has reduced a little and is a good consistency.

Carve the brisket and serve it up with the gravy, some roast potatoes (see p.101) and greens.

Brisket in Mustard Sauce

SERVES 8–10
2kg beef brisket
   in one piece
1 tbsp dry mustard powder
1 tbsp sugar
1 tbsp white wine vinegar
2 bay leaves
1 tsp black peppercorns

Mustard sauce
4 tbsp English
   mustard powder
2 tbsp plain flour
1 tbsp sugar
2 tbsp wholegrain mustard
juice of 1 lemon
75ml white wine vinegar
150g mayonnaise

This might sound quite strange but it really works. The sauce suddenly appears and is wonderfully creamy and delicious. Any leftovers make a great sandwich.

Put the piece of brisket in a large saucepan and cover it with cold water. Add the mustard powder, sugar, vinegar, bay leaves and peppercorns, then bring to the boil. Cover the pan and simmer the meat gently for 3–4 hours, until it is soft and tender but still sliceable. Top the water up every now and again, using just-boiled water. When the meat is done, leave it to cool for 5 minutes.

Preheat the oven to 200°C/Fan 180°C/Gas 6. Carve the meat and put the slices in a large ovenproof dish.

To make the sauce, put the mustard powder and flour in a small pan and slowly stir in 250ml water. Bring to a simmer and continue to stir for 5 minutes. Remove the pan from the heat and stir in the sugar, wholegrain mustard, lemon juice, vinegar and mayonnaise, then pour the sauce over the brisket. Put the dish of brisket in the oven and bake for 30 minutes until bubbling. Serve with seasonal greens.

Porcupine Meatballs

SERVES 6

2 medium carrots, peeled
1 onion, peeled
50g basmati rice
1kg beef mince
2 x 400g cans of cream
    of tomato soup
small bunch of basil,
    leaves picked
extra virgin olive oil
salt and black pepper

No porcupines are used in this recipe! The reason for the name is that as the balls cook, the grains of rice stick out like little porcupine quills.

Coarsely grate the carrots and onion and put them in a bowl with the rice and mince. Season generously, then mix everything together really well. Your hands are best for this. Shape the mixture into about 32 balls – they should be a bit smaller than golf balls.

Pour the tomato soup into a large saucepan, add 500ml of water and bring to the boil. Put the meatballs snugly into the bubbling soup, then pop the lid on the pan and simmer for 20 minutes until the meatballs are cooked through. Serve scattered with basil and drizzled with a little olive oil.

The Perfect Steak

SERVES 4

4 good-quality fillet
   or sirloin steaks
vegetable oil
salt and black pepper

It's vital for steaks to be at room temperature before you start to cook them, otherwise the cooking times won't work and your steak won't be good. It's also really important to let the steaks rest after cooking, so don't be tempted to skip this step. Try the yummy sauces on the opposite page (they also work well with roast beef fillet).

Rub each steak liberally with oil, then season with plenty of salt and pepper. Leave them to sit at room temperature for 30 minutes.

Heat a large frying or griddle pan over a high heat. When the pan begins to smoke it's hot enough for cooking the steaks. Add a couple of the steaks and cook them for 2 minutes on each side for medium-rare meat.

Remove the steaks from the pan, put them on a plate or board and leave them to rest for 15 minutes while you cook the other steaks. Slice and serve with one of the sauces.

Pepper Sauce

SERVES 4
splash of oil
1 onion, peeled and
  finely chopped
2 red peppers, deseeded
  and finely sliced
2 yellow peppers, deseeded
  and finely sliced
1 garlic clove, peeled
  and finely chopped
2 tbsp each of HP sauce,
  A1 Steak sauce, ketchup,
  and Worcestershire
  sauce
a good pinch of Knorr
  Aromat Seasoning

Heat the oil in a frying pan over a medium heat. Add the chopped onion and fry it gently for 5 minutes to soften.

Add the peppers and garlic and continue to cook for 10–15 minutes to soften and caramelize, then put the remaining ingredients into the pan. Bring the sauce to a simmer and let it bubble for another 5 minutes. Remove the pan from the heat, then serve the sauce with the steaks.

Peppercorn Sauce

SERVES 4
knob of butter
  or splash of oil
½ onion, peeled
  and chopped
150g jar of whole
  peppercorns (green
  or black) in brine
600ml double cream
  (or cream alternative)
1½ tsp cracked black
  pepper
salt

Heat the butter or oil in a frying pan over a medium heat. This sauce cooks quickly so you can use the pan you cooked the steaks in – adds flavour and saves on washing up.

Fry the chopped onion for 8–10 minutes until softened, then add the peppercorns, with a splash of their liquid, and the cream to the pan. Bring to a boil, then simmer the sauce for a minute or two to reduce and thicken slightly. Stir in the black pepper, season with salt and serve with the steaks.

Sweet Things

Apple Cake

SERVES 8

120g caster sugar
120g unsalted butter,
   softened
2 large eggs
175g self-raising flour
splash of whole milk
   (optional)
2 large Granny Smith
   apples (about 250g)
1 tbsp cinnamon
2 tbsp demerara sugar

This cake works well with dairy-free butter substitute so it's a good one to make if you're lactose intolerant.

Preheat the oven to 200°C/Fan 180°C/Gas 6. Grease a 20cm loose-bottomed cake tin and line it with baking parchment.

First you need to cream the sugar and butter – make the sure the butter is at room temperature and nice and soft. Put them in a bowl and beat with an electric whisk really thoroughly until the mixture is pale and fluffy. Then whisk in the eggs, one at a time, making sure each egg is well mixed in before adding the next. Sift the flour into the bowl and fold it in gently. If the mixture feels too stiff, add a splash of milk to loosen it a little.

Peel, core and slice the apples, then toss them with the cinnamon. Add about one-quarter of the apple slices to the cake mixture and fold them in gently, then scrape everything into the prepared cake tin. Spread the mixture evenly over the base of the tin, pile in the remaining apple slices, then sprinkle the demerara sugar over the top.

Bake the cake for 30–40 minutes, checking it with a skewer after 30 minutes. If the skewer comes out clean when you insert it into the centre, the cake is done. If there's some mixture clinging to the skewer, pop the cake back into the oven for another 5–10 minutes.

Leave the cake to cool in the tin for 10 minutes, then lift it out of the tin and set it on a wire rack to cool for a little longer. Enjoy while still warm with some vanilla ice cream.

Shally's Sticky Toffee Pudding

SERVES 8–10

225g Medjool dates,
    stoned and roughly
    chopped
1 tsp bicarbonate of soda
100g butter, plus extra
    for greasing
200g caster sugar
2 eggs
2 tbsp golden syrup
275g plain flour
1 tsp baking powder

Brandy sauce
175g soft light
    brown sugar
60ml brandy
30g butter
1 tsp vanilla extract

This is such a great pudding. We like it cold, but when it's hot it goes to another level.

Put the dates in a bowl with the bicarbonate, cover them with 300ml just-boiled water, then leave to soak for about 10 minutes. Preheat the oven to 210°C/Fan 190°C/Gas 6–7.

Cream the butter and sugar thoroughly until really light and fluffy, using a hand-held whisk or a food mixer. Beat in the eggs, one at a time, followed by the golden syrup and the date mixture. Sift the flour and baking powder into the mixture and fold them in gently.

Grease a 2-litre ovenproof dish. Pour the batter into the dish and bake in the oven for 30–40 minutes or until a skewer inserted into the centre comes out clean.

While the pudding is in the oven, make the brandy sauce. Put the sugar, brandy, butter and vanilla in a saucepan and add 200ml water. Bring to the boil, stirring continuously, then let it all bubble for 5 minutes.

When the pudding is ready, pierce lots of holes in the top with a skewer. Pour the sweet sauce over the top and then serve at once.

Jam Biscuits

MAKES 16

250g plain flour,
   plus extra for dusting
125g butter
100g caster sugar, plus
   extra for sprinkling
1 egg, lightly beaten
1 tsp vanilla extract
1 x 454g jar of apricot jam

**Our dad loves these biscuits and will eat loads.
You turn your back and they're all gone!**

Preheat the oven to 200°C/Fan 180°C/Gas 6. Grease a
20 x 30cm baking tray and line it with parchment paper.

Put the flour, butter and sugar in a bowl and rub them
together with your fingers until the mixture looks like
breadcrumbs. Add the beaten egg and vanilla extract,
then mix and bring everything together with your hands
to form a soft dough. Wrap the dough in cling film and
put it in the fridge for 30 minutes – chilling the dough
makes it easier to work with.

Cut one-third off your dough and set it aside. Dust your
work surface with flour, then roll out the larger piece to the
same size as your baking tray. Carefully transfer the dough
to the baking tray, using your fingers to push it into the
edges. Spoon the apricot jam over the dough, making
sure you spread right to the edges.

Coarsely grate the smaller piece of dough and scatter it
over the jam. Bake for 20–25 minutes until the top is golden.

Remove the tray from the oven and leave the biscuits to
cool for 15 minutes. Cut into pieces while the biscuits are
still warm, then put them on a wire rack and leave them
to cool completely before eating.

Custard Biscuits

MAKES 35–40
65g butter
65g caster sugar
1 egg
125g plain flour
70g custard powder
½ tsp baking powder

Icing
180g Bourneville
   chocolate
2 tbsp butter

Mom used to make hundreds of these. Our job, when we were kids, was to match pairs and pass them to mom to sandwich together with chocolate. You can also store the plain biscuits in an airtight container or freeze them.

Preheat the oven to 200°C/Fan 180°C/Gas 6. Line a couple of baking trays with baking parchment.

Cream the butter and sugar until really light and fluffy, using a hand-held whisk or in a food mixer, then beat in the egg. Sift the flour, custard powder and baking powder into a bowl, then carefully fold them into butter mixture.

Take small teaspoonfuls of dough and roll them into balls of about 4 grams. They do rise so will be bigger than you think. Place these on the lined baking trays, spacing them out well, then gently push each one down with a fork. Bake the biscuits in the oven for 6–8 minutes, keeping a close eye on them so they don't burn. Put them on a wire rack to cool completely.

To make the icing, break the chocolate into chunks and put them in a bowl with the butter over a pan of simmering water – the bottom of the bowl shouldn't touch the water. Stir occasionally and when the chocolate and butter have melted, carefully remove the bowl.

Match up the biscuits into pairs of similar sizes. Dip the flat side of one of each pair into the chocolate, then stick it on to its partner. Continue until you've used all the biscuits.

A Peek Up Her Skirt

* *

Mom was very arty and a very original thinker. She was always making something – little dolls, decorations, clothes. While I was collecting things she made to show Jinny, the editor of this book, I discovered this doll that my mom had made for me. I remembered that she sometimes used to sew underwear on her dolls so I had a peak up her skirt. To my surprise, there was a note from my mother. It read: To Dani ... love you. You're special ... be strong ... live, love, laugh xxx. (Dani)

Cinnamon Bulkas

MAKES 16

2 x 7g sachets of
   fast-acting dried yeast
1 tsp caster sugar
1kg bread flour
2 tsp salt
175g sugar, plus
   2 tbsp extra
75g butter, plus 1 tbsp,
   plus extra for greasing
250ml milk
125ml cream
3 eggs
2 tbsp cinnamon

Crumble
100g unsalted butter,
   chilled and diced
200g flour
1 tbsp cinnamon
2 tbsp caster sugar

These are best enjoyed warm, with lots of butter.

Mix the yeast and the teaspoon of caster sugar in a bowl
with 75ml of warm water and leave for a few minutes to
bubble. Put the flour, salt and 175g of sugar in the bowl of
a free-standing food mixer and make a well in the centre.
Put the butter in a small pan with the milk and place the pan
over a gentle heat. When the butter has just melted, add the
cream, remove the pan from the heat and pour the contents
into the bowl with the flour. Add the yeast mixture too.

Whisk the eggs with an electric whisk until bubbly
and full of air, then add them to the mixture.

Using the kneading attachment, gently mix everything
together to form a soft dough – you might need more flour
or liquid at this stage but see how things go. Knead the
dough for 5 minutes until it's smooth and elastic. Cover the
bowl with a piece of oiled cling film and place it somewhere
warm for the dough to prove.

Once the dough has doubled in size, tip it on to a lightly
floured surface and knock it back. Divide the dough into
16 balls, then flatten them so they are about 1–2cm thick.

Melt the extra tablespoon of butter and put it in a small
bowl. Mix the cinnamon and extra sugar together in
another bowl. Grease a 35 x 25cm baking tray.

Brush each bulka with melted butter and sprinkle them
with the cinnamon sugar. Then carefully cut halfway into
the centre of each bulka. Fold the left side on to itself, then
roll towards the right side to create a flower effect. Place
the bulkas into the greased baking tray, cover them with
greased cling film and leave them in a warm place for
30 minutes to an hour, until they have doubled in size.

Preheat the oven to 200°C/Fan 180°C/Gas 6. To make
the crumble topping, put the diced butter in a bowl. Add the
flour and rub the butter and flour together with your fingers
until the mixture looks like breadcrumbs, then stir in the
cinnamon and sugar.

When the bulkas have doubled in size, brush them with
more melted butter and scatter the crumble topping over
them. Bake in the oven for 15–20 minutes – if they start
looking too brown, cover them with foil.

Cheat's Millefeuille

SERVES 6–8

flour, for dusting
350g all-butter puff pastry
80g packet of Osem vanilla
    instant pudding
500ml double cream
250g strawberries, hulled
150g dark chocolate
    (70% cocoa solids)
100g icing sugar

Proper millefeuille is a classic French pastry made with crème pâtissière and takes a while to make! Mom's cheat version is much quicker and still really good to eat.

Preheat the oven to 200°C/Fan 180°C/Gas 6. Line a large baking sheet with baking parchment – you need to have another baking sheet of the same size to hand.

Dust your work surface with flour, then roll out the pastry to make a rectangle measuring about 30 x 40cm. Trim to neaten the edges, then cut the pastry into thirds widthways to make 3 equal rectangles. Place these on the lined baking sheet and prick them all over with a fork, then put the other baking sheet on top so the pastry doesn't puff up too much. Bake the pastry in the oven for 15–20 minutes until cooked and golden, then leave to cool.

Whisk the vanilla pudding mixture in a bowl with the cream. Cut up half the strawberries and fold them into the pudding mixture, then place it in the fridge to firm up for 10 minutes. Slice the remaining strawberries.

Place a piece of pastry on a serving dish or board and spread it with half the vanilla and strawberry mixture. Add a few sliced strawberries, then top with a second piece of pastry. Spread over the remaining vanilla pudding, add more strawberries, then top with the third piece of pastry.

Break up the chocolate and put it in a heatproof bowl. Set the bowl over a pan of simmering water – making sure the bottom of the bowl doesn't touch the water. When the chocolate has melted, carefully remove the bowl from the pan and leave the chocolate to cool slightly.

Mix together the icing sugar with 2 tablespoons of water to make a thick icing. Spread this over the top piece of pastry. Put the melted chocolate in a piping bag and pipe stripes over the icing.

Carefully drag a knife along the top of the millefeuille to create a zig-zag effect in the chocolate. Cut the millefeuille into sections with a sharp knife.

Mom's Own Phone Box

·*·

When we heard that BT was selling off old phone boxes mom decided she had to have one. The box was delivered to our house on a truck and was to be lifted by crane. These things are seriously heavy and weigh at least a tonne.

Mom wanted the box put in front of the window where she could see it easily. But as the guy started to move the truck so he could place it where she'd said, the truck started to tilt – unbalanced by the weight of the box maybe. He swiftly dumped the box at the side of the drive and drove off. We can't move it so there it stays.

Crunchies

MAKES ABOUT 16

375g butter
2 tbsp golden syrup
250g brown sugar
500g rolled oats
225g plain flour
1 tsp bicarbonate of soda
200g desiccated coconut

We used to make loads of these and store them in a tin so when people came over there was always something for them to enjoy with a cup of tea.

Preheat the oven to 200°C/Fan 180°C/Gas 6. Grease a 20 x 20cm baking tray and line it with baking parchment.

Put the butter, syrup and sugar in a large saucepan and place it over a low heat. When everything has melted, take the pan off the heat and add the oats, flour, bicarb and coconut. Stir until well combined. Pour the mixture into the prepared tin and bake for 20 minutes until the edges are just turning golden.

Remove the crunchies from the oven and leave them to cool for 10 minutes. Cut them into squares while still warm.

Date Biscuit Balls

MAKES LOTS

100g Rich Tea biscuits
100g butter
100g caster sugar
250g dates, stoned
   and roughly chopped
50g pecan nuts,
   roughly chopped
1 tsp ground ginger
½ tsp vanilla extract
1 egg, beaten
100g desiccated coconut

"I'm a useless cook. I burn water. But I loved to make a treat called date biscuit balls and mom would talk me through it. I'd be in the kitchen and I'd be pouring sugar or something and, although I didn't think she could see what I was doing, she would know just when to shout 'Stop!' She seemed to smell it in the air." (Megan)

Put the biscuits in a plastic bag, seal it securely and bash the biscuits until they're well crushed. Put the butter and sugar in a large saucepan and place over a low heat until the butter has melted and the sugar dissolved. Stir in the crushed biscuits, dates, pecans and ginger.

Take the pan off the heat and let the mixture cool slightly, then add the vanilla and the beaten egg. Put the pan back on the heat and stir continuously for 3 minutes – take care that the mixture doesn't catch on the bottom of the pan. Remove the pan from the heat.

When the mixture is cool enough to handle, roll it into balls about the size of walnuts. Spread the coconut on a plate and roll the balls in the coconut to coat them. Leave them to cool completely before eating.

Megan's Chocolate Mousse

SERVES 8–10

2 x 180g slabs of
   Bourneville chocolate
50g butter
6 eggs, separated
6 tbsp caster sugar
600ml double cream

If you have any Crunchies or other chocolate bars in your cupboard, crumble them on top of the mousse to add extra texture and flavour. Amazing!

Break the chocolate up into pieces and put them in a large heatproof bowl with the butter. Place the bowl over a pan of simmering water – making sure the bottom of the bowl doesn't touch the water – until the chocolate and butter have melted, stirring occasionally. Carefully remove the bowl from the pan.

Using a free-standing mixer or a hand whisk, beat the egg yolks with 5 tablespoons of the sugar for 5 minutes until the mixture is creamy and pale. (When the whisk is removed, it should leave a trail of batter on the surface.) Stir the melted chocolate into the egg mixture, making sure everything is well incorporated.

In a separate bowl, beat the egg whites to soft peaks, then add the remaining sugar and continue to whisk until stiff.

In another bowl, whisk the cream until it's just holding its shape – be careful not to overwhip it at this stage. Carefully fold the chocolate mix into the cream. Then, using a metal spoon, fold in the egg whites a little at a time, being careful not to knock the air out of the mixture. When everything is combined, pour the mixture into a trifle dish and chill it in the fridge for at least 5 hours or overnight before serving.

Baked Cheesecake

SERVES 8

200g Rich Tea biscuits
120g butter
150g golden caster sugar
500g cream cheese
500g mascarpone cheese
2 large eggs, beaten
2 tsp vanilla extract
    or the seeds from
    1 vanilla pod
finely grated zest
    of 1 lemon
squeeze of lemon juice
icing sugar, for dusting

This is a great-tasting cheesecake. You can also bake the filling in an ovenproof dish, then just spoon it out to serve as a pudding.

Preheat the oven to 190°C/Fan 170°C/Gas 5. Grease a 20cm springform cake tin and line the base with some baking parchment.

Put the biscuits in a food processor and blitz them to fine crumbs. Melt the butter in a saucepan, then stir in the biscuit crumbs. Tip this mixture into the prepared tin and smooth it to the edges with a spoon.

In a free-standing mixer or with a hand whisk, beat the sugar with the cream cheese and mascarpone. Add the eggs, vanilla and lemon zest, then a squeeze of lemon juice and stir to combine. Carefully pour the mixture on to the biscuit base and gently shake the tin to level the top.

Bake the cheesecake for 1 hour, covering the top with foil if it starts to look too brown. At the end of the hour, turn the oven off and leave the cake in the oven for 2 more hours until cooked through.

Take the cake out of the oven and leave it to cool completely. Remove it from tin and dust the top with a little icing sugar before serving.

Flambé Bananas

6 bananas (ripe
    but not too soft)
50g butter
50g soft brown sugar
brandy
ice cream, to serve

This is the simplest pudding but when you light the brandy it looks so dramatic. People think it's the best thing ever. Best to cook the bananas in two batches so you don't overcrowd the pan.

Peel the bananas and cut them in half lengthways. Melt half the butter in a large frying pan over a high heat.

When the butter has melted, stir in half the sugar and allow it to melt. Add half the bananas, cut-side down, then let them caramelize for a couple of minutes. Quickly flip them over and add a good splash of brandy.

Gently tip the pan so the brandy catches the flame – or light the brandy with a match – and cook for 1 minute, letting the flame burn off. Take care doing this and don't get anything else, such as a tea towel – or your hair – near the flame.

Tip the bananas on to serving plates, then cook the rest. Add good dollops of ice cream before serving.

Tiramisu

SERVES 8
4 egg yolks
4 tbsp caster sugar
500g mascarpone cheese
250ml double cream
300ml strong
    sweetened coffee
200g packs Savoiardi
    sponge fingers
cocoa powder

This is very rich so it's good for an occasional treat. We always present it in a beautiful glass bowl and it looks amazing. Nice with some berries or other fruit on the side.

Put the egg yolks and sugar in a large bowl and whisk them together for 5 minutes until the mixture is really pale and voluminous. You can use a hand-held whisk or a food mixer to do this.

Whisk the mascarpone in a separate bowl to loosen it slightly, then fold into the egg mixture, a little at a time. Beat the cream until it has thickened slightly, then fold it into the egg mix. Pour the sweetened coffee into a separate bowl.

You need a large serving bowl. Dip one-third of the biscuits into the coffee and use them to line the bottom of the bowl. Spoon one-third of the egg, mascarpone and cream mixture over the biscuits, taking care to spread it all over them, then sieve some cocoa powder on top. Repeat these layers twice more, making sure you have a generous layer of cocoa powder on top. Pop the tiramisu in the fridge and leave it to chill for at least 2 hours before serving.

Pavlova

SERVES 8–10

8 egg whites, at room
  temperature
pinch of salt
400g caster sugar
1 tbsp cornflour
2 tsp vanilla extract
  or the seeds from
  1 vanilla pod

Topping

500ml double cream
80g packet Osem vanilla
  instant pudding
500g ripe strawberries,
  hulled
mix of redcurrants,
  blueberries, blackberries
  or other seasonal fruit

This is perfect for a party, as it looks so spectacular and everyone loves it. You can make the meringue base the night before and just add the filling at the last moment.

Preheat the oven to 160°C/Fan 140°C/Gas 3. Draw a 25cm circle on a piece of baking parchment and place it on a baking sheet. If you don't have a baking sheet big enough, then line an oven shelf with foil.

Using a free-standing mixer, or a hand-held whisk, beat the egg whites until they form soft peaks. Whisking constantly, add a pinch of salt and the sugar, a tablespoon at a time, until it is all in and the mixture is really stiff and glossy. Check that the sugar has dissolved into the egg whites by rubbing a little of the mixture between your fingers. If it feels smooth it is ready; if it is still a little grainy, continue to whisk until it is smooth.

Fold the cornflour and vanilla into the meringue with a large metal spoon. Pile the meringue on top of the baking parchment, trying to fit it in the shape of the circle you drew. Pop the meringue into the oven and bake it for 2 hours, then turn the oven off and leave it for another hour. Take the meringue out of the oven and leave it to cool completely.

When you're ready to eat, whip the cream and vanilla pudding until the mixture is just holding its shape, then spoon it on to the meringue. Cut the strawberries in halves or quarters and pile them on to the cream. Add more berries if you like and serve at once.

Chocolate Chiffon Cake

250g caster sugar
250g plain flour
3 tbsp cocoa powder
pinch of salt
pinch of cinnamon
3½ tsp baking powder
8 eggs
160ml vegetable oil
250ml just-boiled water
icing sugar, for dusting
   (optional)

**Chocolate buttercream
   icing**
500g butter
1kg icing sugar
4 tbsp cocoa powder
1 tsp vanilla essence
splash of milk

A chiffon cake is the lightest and fluffiest of cakes. It contains no raising agents – it is the large quantity of egg whites that make it rise. You mustn't grease the tin, as this delicate cake needs to cling to the sides so it doesn't collapse in the oven.

Preheat the oven to 200°C/Fan 180°C/Gas 6. Put the sugar, flour, cocoa powder, salt, cinnamon and 2½ teaspoons of the baking powder in a large mixing bowl (or in the bowl of a free-standing mixer).

Separate the eggs and put the 8 whites in a large bowl and 7 of the yolks in another bowl.

Make a well in the centre of the dry ingredients and add the yolks, oil and just-boiled water. Whisk for 6–7 minutes until the batter is voluminous and thoroughly combined. Whisk the whites with the remaining teaspoon of baking powder until they form soft peaks.

Slowly pour the batter into the egg whites and carefully fold them together with a large metal spoon. Make sure you mix the egg whites in thoroughly but take care not to knock the air out.

Carefully pour the batter into a large chiffon tin – do not grease the tin. Bake the cake for an hour.

Remove the cake from the oven. Now this next bit will sound very odd but it's important and it works. Turn the tin upside down and place it on a Worcestershire sauce bottle – it's the perfect size. It's vital that you cool the cake facing downwards in this way, as otherwise it will sink.

Leave the cake to cool completely. To remove it, very carefully run a knife between the cake and the tin to release the cake from the sides, then turn it out. Ice the cake or simply dust it with icing sugar.

To make the icing, cream the butter and icing sugar, then sift in the cocoa powder and mix well. Add the vanilla essence and a little milk to get a good silky consistency.

A Lady
with a Big Heart

∗•∗

In 2002 I came from Zimbabwe to work at the King Edward VII hospital in London. Shally was a patient there when I started and she heard my voice in the corridor. She recognized my accent and asked someone about me; she said she wanted to meet me.

When I went to see her she wanted to know all about me, my life and my family. I explained that I'd had to leave my kids behind and as a mother herself she knew how very hard that was for me. We talked and talked about home, about what we missed, the African foods we loved. She could see how desperately homesick I was and she loved how my mouth started watering when we talked about our favourite dishes.

A few days after our first meeting I got a call from reception to say there was a big parcel waiting for me. It was a food hamper from Shally, packed with biltong, dried guava and other South African delicacies. It was amazing and it helped me feel at home. Those foods brought back so many memories.

We became the best of friends and shared so much. When she was ill I sometimes had to be cruel to be kind in order to get her to follow her treatment. She would lose her appetite and not want to eat but I would tell her, "Eat for me. It's like taking your medicine and it's important. You need to eat so you can get strong and get back to your family."

Some years later she came to see me when I was ill in hospital. She asked me if I had an appetite – I didn't. She herself was in a wheelchair then, but she prepared food and brought it to me. She told me I had to eat it – she gave me a taste of my own medicine!

Shally was a lady with a big heart. She cared about everyone. Even from her sickbed she would always take everyone else's problems to heart. They became her problems and she would offer any help she could. When my father was dying, she was there for me, holding my hands and crying with me. When my kids did well she rejoiced for them and for me.

When she was in hospital she would always go the extra mile to show her appreciation for all the staff. And not just the doctors. She would get gifts for the receptionists and the porters, for the people who served her meals. She knew everyone and always addressed them by name. She really cared about people.

Shally was never rude or inconsiderate. Despite what she was going through herself, she never lost her love for people. She always focused on the positive and would never dwell on bad news for long. She wanted to get the very best from life.

Every day, I think of Shally and what she would do if she were here. She will always be in my heart. (Sibo Sibanda)

Creamy Mango Pudding

3 ripe mangoes
250ml double cream
250g thick plain yoghurt
squeeze of lime juice
100g muscovado sugar

Be sure to use muscovado sugar here, not ordinary brown sugar. The muscovado reacts with the creamy mix and becomes caramelized – a bit like a brûlée topping.

Peel and slice the mangoes, discarding the stones. Put the slices in the base of a medium-sized trifle bowl.

In a large bowl, whip the cream until it's just holding its shape. Fold in the yoghurt and stir in the lime juice. Spoon the cream over the fruit, then sprinkle the sugar in a thin layer on top.

Pop the dish into the fridge for 2–3 hours. It's ready when the sugar has dissolved on the surface and looks melted and gorgeously gooey.

Honey Cake

3 eggs, beaten
120g brown sugar
150ml sunflower oil
350g honey
200g golden syrup
350g self-raising flour
1½ tsp ground ginger
1½ tsp cinnamon
1½ tsp bicarbonate of soda
dash of vanilla extract
2 tsp cocoa powder
200ml boiled water,
   cooled to warm
honey, to glaze
   (as much as you want)

This cake is best made in a special bundt tin. This usually has fluted sides but the most important thing is the tube or chimney in the centre, which distributes heat more evenly through the cake as it bakes. Be generous with the honey – we sometimes pour a whole pot over this cake.

Preheat the oven to 190°C/Fan 170°C/Gas 5. Add all the ingredients, except the water and the extra honey for glazing, to a large bowl and stir well to combine. Then add the warm water and mix to make a lovely smooth batter.

Pour the batter into the bundt tin and bake the cake in the preheated oven for 40 minutes.

Remove the cake from the oven, let it cool slightly, then turn it on to a serving plate. Warm the honey for the glaze in a small pan, then brush some over the cake. Pour the rest over the top.

Clowning Around

·*·

Kids' parties were a riot in our house and mom would make really fun things for us to eat. For the racing cars, use finger biscuits for the base, then add white chocolate buttons for wheels. Decorate your cars with sprinkles and sweeties to make them as fancy as you like. For the clowns, put an ice-cream cone upside down on a biscuit and fix it in place with icing. Decorate with Smarties and icing – let your imagination run wild.

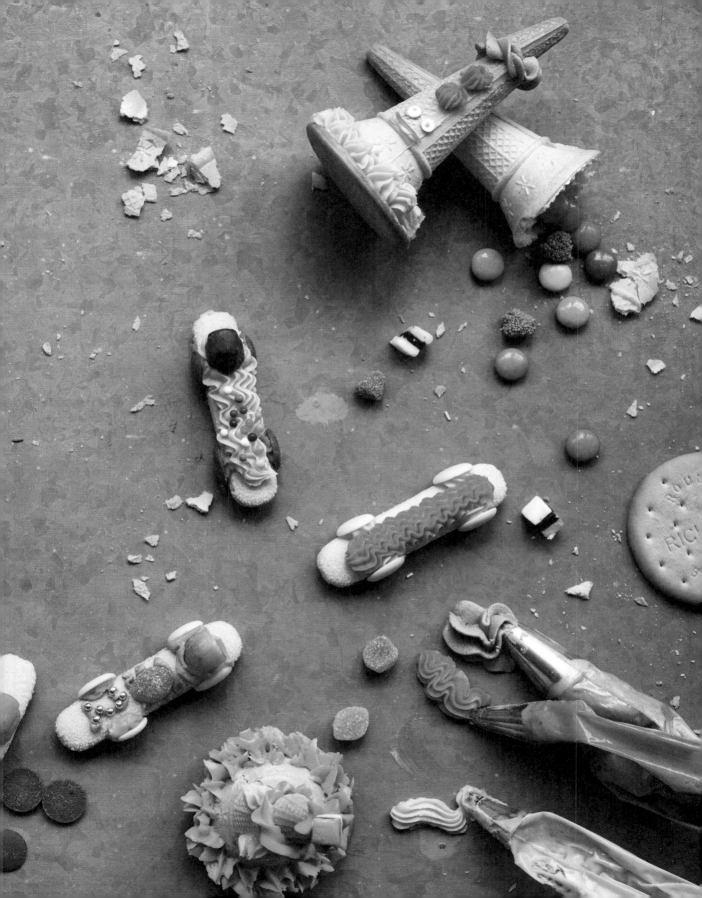

Greek Nut Biscuits

MAKES 30–35
BISCUITS
250g butter, room
temperature
300g icing sugar
200g plain flour
125g pecan nuts,
chopped
2 tsp vanilla extract

Make these lovely crumbly little biscuits bite-size so you can pop them straight into your mouth – otherwise the icing sugar gets all over your clothes!

Cream the butter with 100g of the icing sugar by hand or in a food mixer. Add the flour, pecans, vanilla and 2 teaspoons of water and mix to a soft dough. Preheat the oven to 200°C/Fan 180°C/Gas 6.

Roll pieces of the dough into small balls – you should have about 30–35 – and place them on a greased baking tray. Bake the biscuits for 15 minutes, then leave them to cool.

When the biscuits are cool, spread the rest of the icing sugar on a plate and roll them in it to coat generously.

Carrot Cake

SERVES 6–8

500g plain flour
2 heaped tsp baking
   powder
1½ tsp bicarbonate
   of soda
1 tsp salt
3 tsp cinnamon
2 tsp ground ginger
500g caster sugar
375ml sunflower oil
4 eggs
500g carrots, peeled
   and grated
250g canned crushed
   pineapple, drained
125g pecan nuts, chopped

Icing
280g cream cheese
125g butter
600g icing sugar
2 tsp vanilla extract

The pineapple in this recipe is what makes it special. You don't really taste it but it makes the cake beautifully moist and juicy.

Preheat the oven to 200°C/Fan 180°C/Gas 6. Grease a 20cm springform tin and line the bottom with baking parchment. Sift the flour, baking powder, bicarbonate of soda, salt, cinnamon and ginger into a bowl. Put the sugar, oil and eggs in a separate bowl and mix well with a hand whisk. Stir the carrots, pineapple and pecans into the egg mixture.

Add half the dry ingredients to the wet and stir well, then mix in the rest. Pour the cake batter into the tin and bake the cake in the preheated oven for 45–60 minutes. Test by inserting a skewer into the centre of the cake. If it comes out clean the cake is done. If not, put it back in the oven for another 5 minutes.

Mix all the ingredients for the icing in a food mixer or in a bowl with a hand whisk. When the cake is cool, cover it with the icing.

Mini Bundt Cakes

MAKES 12
125g butter, room
    temperature
100g Philadelphia
    cream cheese
175g caster sugar
2 eggs
135g self-raising flour
½ tsp vanilla extract

Icing
50g butter, room
    temperature
100g icing sugar,
    plus extra to sieve
100g Philadelphia
    cream cheese

Ideally, these should be baked in mini bundt tins, which have little 'chimneys' in the middle just like the full-size ones (see page 214).

Preheat the oven to 190°C/Fan 170°C/Gas 5. Put 95g of the butter in a bowl and soften it with a whisk, then add the cream cheese and beat until smooth. Add the sugar and beat again, then add the eggs one at a time, beating each one in well until you have a smooth batter. Sieve the flour into a bowl and fold it into the batter, then stir the vanilla extract.

Melt the remaining butter and use it to brush the insides of 12 mini bundt tins. Divide the batter between the tins – you might find it easier to spoon the batter into a piping bag and pipe it into each tin. Pop the cakes into the oven and bake them for 12–15 minutes.

When the cakes are done, remove them from the oven and leave them to cool in the tins for a couple of minutes. Then tip the cakes out on to a cooling rack and leave to cool completely.

To make the icing, beat the butter until it's soft, then add the icing sugar a little at a time. Slowly mix in the cream cheese to make an icing with a lovely runny consistency. Drizzle the cakes with the icing or simply dust them with icing sugar – whatever you prefer.

Apple Crumble

SERVES 6–8
250g plain flour
½ tsp salt
125g butter, diced
4 tsp cinnamon
150g brown sugar
8 apples (mixture of
    eating and cooking)

Custard
500ml milk
100g caster sugar
2 tbsp cornflour
1 tbsp plain flour
2 egg yolks
1 whole egg
1 tsp vanilla extract

Everyone loves a crumble and this is mom's version, always served with a big jug of home-made custard.

Preheat the oven to 200°C/Fan 180°C/Gas 6. Put the flour, salt and diced butter in a bowl with 2 teaspoons of the cinnamon and half the brown sugar. Rub everything together with your fingertips until the mixture is the consistency of breadcrumbs.

Peel the apples, cut them into quarters, then remove the cores and slice. Put them in a baking dish and sprinkle the crumble mixture on top to completely cover the fruit.

Mix the rest of the cinnamon and sugar together and sprinkle them over the crumble. Pop the dish in the oven and bake for about 25 minutes, then serve hot with custard.

CUSTARD

To make the custard, pour 375ml of the milk into a saucepan and place it over a low heat. Meanwhile, put the sugar, cornflour and flour in a bowl and whisk in the remaining 125ml of milk. Whisk in the egg yolks, then crack in the whole egg and add the vanilla. Whisk again until everything is well combined.

When the milk is just about boiling, slowly add the egg mixture, while whisking. Keep whisking for a couple of minutes over a low heat until you see the mixture thicken and start to look like custard. Great served hot or cold.

Cheese Blintzes

SERVES 4–6

3 large eggs
225g plain flour
½ tsp baking powder
salt
butter, for frying

Filling

250g cream cheese
1 large egg
pinch of cinnamon
50 golden caster sugar

This is Great Granny Becca's recipe. She would always make these when we went to visit and we LOVED them.

Crack the eggs into a large bowl, add 200ml cold water and beat well. Sift the flour, baking powder and a good pinch of salt and mix them into the eggs well. Leave the batter to rest for an hour.

Heat a large frying pan over a medium heat and grease it lightly with a little butter. Add a ladleful of batter, then tip the pan around so the batter spreads over the bottom of the pan. Cook for about 2 minutes, then carefully loosen the pancake, flip it over and cook it for another minute or so. Put it on a warm plate, then continue until you've used up all the batter. Put the grill on to preheat to medium.

To make the filling, beat together the cream cheese, egg, cinnamon and a pinch of sugar to taste. Spoon a small amount of filling on to each pancake then roll them up, placing them in an ovenproof dish. Sprinkle them with the remaining sugar and place under the grill for 5 minutes or until the filling is hot and the sugar caramelized on top. Enjoy immediately.

Fabric Sweets

✳·✳

Our mom used to love to make these little fabric "sweeties" to decorate the table or to give as presents to friends. She would choose little scraps of fabric, buttons, ribbons and sequins from her treasure chest and make every one different. To make some yourself, get some cross-stitch material and cover it with coloured stitching or choose a lovely scrap of fabric. Sew it up, stuff it with wadding – you could add a few drops of scented oil – then decorate with any embellishments you like.

Live. Love. Laugh.

Someone once said that pain is inevitable, but suffering is optional. We feel so honoured and privileged to say that our mom didn't just speak these words, she lived by them too.

Our lives are not determined by what happens to us but how we react to what happens; not by what life brings to us, but by the attitude we bring to life. A positive attitude causes a chain reaction of positive thoughts, events and outcomes. It is a catalyst, a spark that creates extraordinary results.

Never once was Shally brought down by pain. There was always laughter and happiness surrounding her. She looked to the light when all that surrounded her was darkness.

We should all attempt to take a chapter out of her life book. While we have lost an incredible and inspiring woman, we must continue to look to the light that surrounds the darkness of her passing.

While it's okay to cry and be upset, it's also important that we giggle, smile and remember what Shally believed in. Life isn't about dwelling on the pain and the suffering but finding the laughter in the saddest of times, the music in the quietest of moments, and the happiness in moments of despair.

Conversion Tables

In this book we use metric measurements, but the following tables give imperial equivalents should you need. Always stick to the same system when following a recipe and never use a mixture of imperial and metric. Some measurements have been rounded up or down for simplicity's sake.

OVEN TEMPERATURES (°Celsius, °Fahrenheit, Gas mark)

°C	Fan oven °C	°F	Gas
110	90	225	¼
120	100	250	½
140	120	275	1
150	130	300	2
160	140	325	3
180	160	350	4
190	170	375	5
200	180	400	6
220	200	425	7
230	210	450	8
240	220	475	9

WEIGHT

Metric (grams and kilograms)	Imperial (ounces and pounds)
25g	1oz
50g	2oz
75g	3oz
100g	4oz
150g	5oz
175g	6oz
200g	7oz
225g	8oz
250g	9oz
275g	10oz
350g	12oz
375g	13oz
400g	14oz
450g	1lb
550g	1lb 4oz
675g	1lb 8oz
750g	1lb 12oz
900g	2lb
1kg	2lb 2oz
1.5kg	3lb

VOLUME

Metric (millilitres and litres)	Imperial (UK fluid ounces and pints)
25ml	1fl oz
50ml	2fl oz
85ml	3fl oz
100ml	3½ fl oz
125ml	4fl oz
150ml	5fl oz
175ml	6fl oz
200ml	7fl oz
225ml	8fl oz
275ml	9fl oz
300ml	10fl oz
450ml	15fl oz
600ml	20fl oz (1 pint)
700ml	1¼ pints
900ml	1½ pints
1 litre	1¾ pints
1.2 litres	2 pints
1.75 litres	3 pints
2.25 litres	4 pints
2.75 litres	5 pints

LENGTH

Metric (centimetres)	Imperial (inches)
1cm	½ in
2.5cm	1in
5cm	2in
7.5cm	3in
10cm	4in
15cm	6in
20cm	8in
25cm	10in
30cm	12in
50cm	20in

Teaspoons and tablespoons

1 teaspoon is 5ml
1 tablespoon is 15ml

American liquid measures

1 US pint is 16 UK fluid ounces (about 475ml)

Index

THANK YOU

Charlie Clapp, you are a culinary genius and have become a dear friend. Dan Jones, with a camera in your hand, you make the world look beautiful. Linda Berlin prop-styling is what you were born to do! Alex Smith and the Smith & Gilmour team – you made this process feel effortless, you are that good at what you do. Jinny Johnson, our editor, you have the extraordinary ability to remain calm, iron out the chaos and bring it all together, faultlessly. To Candice Rakusin at R6 for your help with the English language. To Simon Mackenzie and to Sophie Fox for assisting us on set, and to Andrew Burton for additional photography and Christina Mackenzie for help with the food shoots.

Professor Malcolm Rustin – your dedication to my mother went well beyond what could ever have been expected. You are a very special human being. For our mom, you led a team of the world's most expert doctors, namely, Dr Huw Beynon, Dr Robin Woolfson, Dr Charlie Murray, Dr Steven Hurel, Dr Norman Johnson, Dr Ian Cropley and Dr Adrian Tookman, and together you gave us the gift of our mother for much longer than we could ever have imagined. There is nothing for which we could be more grateful.

Matron Caroline Cassels, you made us feel like we were a part of the King Edward VII Hospital family. You and your team managed to provide us with comfort and reassurance during our most challenging times but you did more than that – you sat with us, you listened, you made us laugh until we cried and when we actually were crying, you made sure that our tears were short-lived. Sibo Sibanda, you are an incredible nurse and a true friend to our family. Our mom was helped and healed by so many extraordinary nurses and doctors: Dr Kojo Ndenecho, Khumo Malete, Bibian Koyi, Melanie Sinclair, Anna Wallis de Garay, Rod Lusterio, Thantaswa Mtshemla, Marlene Noel, Lisa Andrew, Faith Van Wyk, Benedictor Phokwana, Jelena Konovalova and Sue Tafeni.

Our mom was privileged to have had an incredible family: her mom, siblings and their families were a constant support in her life and remain so in ours. To our extended family and friends – it is because of you that our kitchen is so social and so full of fun, love and deliciousness. Our mom absolutely adored each and every one of you, as do we.

To our grandfather, Mikey, your love and generosity is limitless and deeply appreciated.

To our dad, Lawrence, you have made this book and everything else in our lives possible. You loved our mother unconditionally, a love we witnessed daily and we will remember always.

And finally, to our mother, Shally – this one is for you. We love you eternally.